THE JUSTICE MEN OWE WOMEN

Titles in
Sacred ✹ Energies
a series from Fortress Press in collaboration with
The Religious Consultation on Population,
Reproductive Health and Ethics

Sacred Energies:
When the World's Religions Sit Down to Talk about the
Future of Human Life and the Plight of This Planet
Daniel C. Maguire
(2000)

Sacred Choices:
The Right to Contraception and Abortion
in Ten World Religions
Daniel C. Maguire
(2001)

The Justice Men Owe Women:
Positive Resources from World Religions
John C. Raines
(2001)

Power, Pleasure, and Justice
Mary E. Hunt and Patricia Beattie Jung
(forthcoming)

THE JUSTICE MEN OWE WOMEN
Positive Resources from World Religions

John C. Raines

Fortress Press
Minneapolis

THE JUSTICE MEN OWE WOMEN
Positive Resources from World Religions
Copyright © 2001 Augsburg Fortress. All rights reserved. Except for brief quotations in critical articles or reviews, no part of this book may be reproduced in any manner without prior written permission from the publisher. Write: Permissions, Augsburg Fortress, Box 1209, Minneapolis, MN 55440.

Cover photograph by Farinaz Taghavi, copyright © 2000 Photodisc, Inc.
Cover design: Marti Naughton
Interior design: Beth Wright

Scripture quotations used by Gerard S. Sloyan are from the New American Standard Bible, copyright © 1960, 1962, 1963, 1968, 1971, 1972, 1973, 1975, 1977 by the Lockman Foundation, and are used by permission.
Scripture quotations used by Marvin Ellison are from the Revised Standard Version of the Bible, copyright © 1946, 1952, 1971 by the Division of Christian Education of the National Council of the Churches of Christ in the USA, and are used by permission. Quotation in chapter 2 from the Gospel of Thomas is reprinted from "The Gospel of Thomas (11,2)," translated by Helmut Koester and Thomas O. Lambdin, in *The Nag Hammadi Library in English*, edited by James M. Robinson (San Francisco: Harper and Row, 1988).
Scripture passages used by Ali Asghar Engineer are from *Holy Qur'an*, translated by M. M. Ali (Pakistan: Lahore, 1973). Farid Esack has provided his own translation of the Arabic text.
Scripture quotations used by Ze'ev Falk are his own translation from the Hebrew. Scripture on pages 52–53 from the New King James Version is copyright © 1979, 1980, 1982, Thomas Nelson, Inc., and is used by permission (all rights reserved).

Library of Congress Cataloging-in-Publication Data

Raines, John C.
    The justice men owe women : positive resources from world religions / John C. Raines.
        p.   cm.
    Includes bibliographical references and index.
    ISBN 0-8006-3281-8 (alk. paper)
    1. Women and religion. 2. Sexism—Religious aspects. 3. Equality—Religious aspects.
    I. Title.
    BL458 .R35 2001
    291.1'78334—dc21

                                                    2001033639

The paper used in this publication meets the minimum requirements of American National Standard for Information Sciences — Permanence of Paper for Printed Library Materials, ANSI Z329.48-1984.

Manufactured in the U.S.A.   AF1-3281
05   04   03   02   01   1   2   3   4   5   6   7   8   9   10

For
Lucille Arnold Raines
and
Helen Latta

O humankind! We have created you all out of a male and a female, and have made you into nations and tribes so that you might come to know one another. Verily, the noblest of you in the sight of God is the one who is most deeply conscious of God.

—*Qur'an* 49:13

Contents

RELIGIONS ARE GENDERED BECAUSE LANGUAGES ARE GENDERED, and we learn our religion by way of language—both written and spoken. More than that, in our practicing of religion, in our praying, in our singing, in our listening to and in our exposition of scripture, we are in the territory of he and of she, of him and of her. The tradition of the sacred is usually a tradition written by men for the eyes and ears of other men. When sacred writings speak of women, it is in the language of "them," hardly ever of "I" or of "you." So why should we bother with religion, which is almost always the voice of patriarchy?

Because even today, in our so-called secular age, religion ultimately steers the world. That appears to be a preposterous claim in a world seemingly steered by money and power. Nevertheless, the worship of money and of power has occasionally been in charge, but only when some other, more vigorous worship has not superseded money and power. The tribal wars in Central Africa and the ethnic conflicts in India or Bosnia illustrate that money and power are not the only forces driving human nature.

We humans are worshiping beings. What our hearts cling to and rely upon not only orders our personal lives but also orders the lives we share with others. To see into the soul of a society, ask about its common worship. Ancient Rome worshiped glory. In the United States, we worship the American Dream—a dream that is only partly about money. Religion is as inevitable as breathing or as the blood that pulses through our veins. We all have hearts; besides beating, they also love and hope and cling. We cannot just discount religion and leave it to others—we leave religion only to worship something else. It is best, therefore, to ask ourselves: Upon what does my heart or our hearts rely? What is my sacred or our sacred?

Religion is both gendered and gendering. What it reflects it recreates. It takes sides; it privileges one gender over another. But sometimes religion also talks about justice. Occasionally it even speaks about the justice we men owe women, although many times this entails men giving other men moral advice, with women being spoken about and waiting offstage. When dealing with the heritage of the sacred, we are dealing with both a presence and an absence. For women to become present in the sacred they must have a say, become an "I" and a "we"—no longer the "them" listening offstage. For men, to search the sacred in our struggle for justice is not to struggle "for them," but to struggle for ourselves, to recover from dishonesty, to hear the unheard male bias in our heritage of worship, and to give clarity to our own hearts and to what they cling to and rely upon.

If part of our task is to unveil the patriarchal bias that embeds itself in the sacred, an even more important task is to sort out the positive resources in our religious traditions that support the idea of equal dignity between men and women. Each of the world religions has a strong theory of fundamental equality and a claim for social justice that follows from it. We will ask, therefore, how our scriptures, how our founding prophets, and how our ancestors can be used today to further justice in relations between the genders.

Furthering justice in relations between the genders is the ambitious task of this book. It will mostly fail, because justice in gender relationships depends less on knowing what is right than on doing what is right. Our doing is always culturally specific; for example, whatever we are led to think or to do in response to the demands of justice in gender relations, most women living in this century will live and die in poverty and so will their children. Certainly, this is true for those already born. There is no dependable evidence that the situation will suddenly change. Indeed, demographic projections predict older and smaller populations in the more wealthy countries, while younger and larger populations will swell the ranks of already impoverished nations. According to the United Nations 1997 Report on the Status of Women, 70 percent of the world's 1.3 billion people living in poverty are women. Every week, a quarter of a million children die from malnutrition or infection.

This book will mostly fail because we cannot avoid these grim prospects, although we can improve upon them. They invite our efforts because small improvements can mean much for those who have little to begin with. For a poor woman to begin with an "I deserve!" spoken from out of her own sacred tradition is a step toward a better future. The voice is there. However overwritten with masculinist ideology, in every religious tradition there is also the voice that invites us into a shared struggle for justice. That struggle is one that we—men and women together—are obliged to join. Well . . . we are only obliged if we agree to be obliged. As the Marquis de Sade reminds us, "You don't have to have a soul unless you want one."

No text appears out of nowhere, and this text has its context. It is a shortened and popularized version of a scholarly volume composed of essays written by ten scholars of world religions—all men. Why all men and why this male author? Because sexism is primarily a problem men have that becomes a problem for women because of the power men have over women's lives. The heritage of our sacred texts speaks in a male voice, usually to our male advantage. We men owe it to ourselves, therefore, to extricate ourselves from this complicity. That at least has been the conviction of the male scholars who will be our guides. In the eight chapters to follow, we will interrogate world religions, asking what each has to say on gender justice and asking why we should pay attention. Just as every culture has its own specific history and development, each chapter stands alone. Taken together, the chapters also tell the story of a connected struggle, the struggle for justice in gender relations under conditions imposed by the new global economy and its winners and losers.

Our guides include Anantanand Rambachan, who teaches Hinduism at Saint Olaf College in Minnesota; Gerard Sloyan, a Roman Catholic New Testament scholar teaching at Catholic University of America; and Marvin Ellison, a Protestant Christian ethicist teaching at Bangor Theological Seminary in Maine. Asghar Ali Engineer and Farid Esack are both Muslim scholars but live in very different countries—India and South Africa, respectively. Ze'ev Falk was an orthodox rabbi teaching at the Seminary of Judaic Studies in Jerusalem. Tavivat Puntarigvivat is a Buddhist activist-scholar teaching in Bangkok. Congolese-born Mutombo Nkulu-N'Sengha teaches African American studies at Temple University. Liu Xiaogan, born in the People's Republic of China, now teaches at the National University of Singapore. Christopher Ronwanien:te Jocks teaches Native American religions at Dartmouth College. (For more information, see the Biographies chapter at the end of the book.) Readers may wish also to consult the fuller study, *What Men Owe to Women: Men's Voices from World Religions*, edited by John C. Raines and Daniel C. Maguire (Albany: SUNY Press, 2001).

While these scholars will act as our guides, I am solely responsible for what they are given the opportunity to say. That has been my choice; in addition, each chapter contains much of my own material. As a group, we are scholars trained in world religions. We have enjoyed extended educations and what that means in terms of relative class privilege. You will hear our voices, not the voices of women, certainly not the voices of poor women who are the majority of women living on planet Earth. You will want to debate with us, with yourself, and among yourselves. Sexism is mostly a male problem imposed upon women because of the power society gives men. Perhaps the most important of those powers is religion. It requires our critical attention. Criticism does not imply disrespect, but care.

Acknowledgments

EVERY BOOK IS PART OF A CONVERSATION. It is born out of conversation and returns itself to that conversation. This is most assuredly the case with the present volume. It was born out of a conversation among eleven male scholars of world religions concerning how their religious traditions were not only conspirators in but also resources of opposition to the domination and exploitation of women. Dan Maguire, President of the Religious Consultation on Population, Reproductive Health and Ethics, inspired the process; in addition, through his skills of persuasion, the Ford, MacArthur, and Packard Foundations funded the project.

This book would not exist in its present form without the vigorous critical responses of feminist scholars Riffat Hassan, Christine Gudorf, Laurie Zoloth-Dorfman, and Eva Neumaier-Dargyay, who early in the process inserted female voices into our male conversations. The manuscript also benefited from critical readings by David Gracie, Irfan Omar, Amy Weigand, Hal Commons, and Edie Giese.

I wrote the book in Jakarta, Indonesia, where I was a Fulbright scholar and lecturer and where, in spite of their deep economic distress, a mostly Muslim people warmly welcomed me. I thank all of the people who played a part in this unfinished conversation.

1. Hinduism

WE BEGIN OUR STORY ABOUT RELIGION AND GENDER JUSTICE as it is told under the guidance of Hinduism. What are the instructions Hindu men receive concerning the proper view of women, and what are Hindu women taught that they should expect from men? One of Hinduism's oldest foundational texts is *The Code of Manu* (c. 2000 B.C.E.). A male text written for a male audience, it gives religious sanction to an attitude that is not uniquely Hindu but that continues to influence that culture.

By a girl, by a young woman, or even by an aged one, nothing must be done independently, even in her own house.

In childhood a female must be subject to her father, in youth to her husband, when her lord is dead to her sons; a woman must never be independent.

Though destitute of virtue, or seeking pleasure (elsewhere), or devoid of good qualities, (yet) a husband must be constantly worshiped as a god by a faithful wife.

No sacrifice, no vow, no fast must be performed by women apart (from their husbands); if a wife obeys her husband, she will for that (reason alone) be exalted in heaven.

A faithful wife, who desires to dwell (after death) with her husband, must never do anything that might displease him who took her hand, whether he be alive or dead.

The subservience, the required obedience, and the ubiquitous surveillance of their lives by their fathers, brothers, husbands, and sons is an early and persisting moral conviction about what Hindu men owe to Hindu women and what Hindu women should expect and accept from men.

If we think that *The Code of Manu* is too ancient to carry cultural weight some four thousand years later, we can consider a more recent text, one that remains a favorite of many today. The sixteenth-century poet Tulasidasa produced a vernacular reworking of the

1

ancient Sanskrit text *Ramayaṇa* of Valniki. Ghandi called it the greatest literature in all world religions. It encodes women, especially women's bodies, with the fears and biases of males who conceive their highest calling to be an ascetic life freed from desire and its attendant illusions, the celibate renunciant or *samnyasi*.

> Lust, wrath, greed, pride, and all other violent passions form the sturdy army of infatuation; but among them all the most formidable and calamitous is woman, illusion incarnate.
>
> Listen sage, the Puranas and Vedas and the saints declare that woman is the vernal season to the forest of infatuation, like the heat of summer she dries up all the ponds and lakes of prayer and penance and devotional exercises.

The trope on women as deserts that suck up and dry out male seminal fluid is widespread in religious literature, not confined to Hinduism.

Such religiously sanctioned attitudes construct a slippery slope down which male anger at women can soon take on the disciplinary practice of physical violence. In a recent and popular tract titled *How to Lead a Household Life*, Swami Ramsukhdas offers the following advice to Hindu women facing an abusing husband:

> QUESTION: What should the wife do if her husband beats her and troubles her?
>
> ANSWER: The wife should think that she is paying her debt of her previous life and thus her sins are being destroyed and she is becoming pure. When her parents come to know this, they can take her to their own house because they have not given their daughter to face this sort of bad behavior.
>
> QUESTION: What should she do if her parents don't take her to their own house?
>
> ANSWER: Under such circumstances what can the helpless wife do? She should reap the fruit of her past actions. She should patiently bear the beatings of her husband with patience. By bearing them she will be free from her sins and it is possible that her husband may start loving her.

Encouraging a passive response by women to the abuse of wife beating can be found sprinkled liberally throughout Eastern and Western religious literatures.

However, it would be a mistake to confine our study of these matters only to the written word. Religion is something more than what we think and write about. It is something we act on. Religion is thoroughly embodied, even if, perhaps especially if, regarded as practiced most perfectly in male asceticism. Religion is a matter of arms and of legs, of feet, tongue, lips, and vocal cords. It is something we do and dance and sing together. As children, we see and hear religion long before we are taught to understand the meaning of what we see and hear. Religion is visible and audible. It is what postmodern social science calls a "practice." If we want to understand a religion—any religion—we must watch it, listen to it, even smell it. And all this is especially true of Hinduism, which presents us with a veritable supermarket of colors and sounds and movements in its rich pageant of sacred ritual.

In its embodiment of the sacred in ritual, Hinduism privileges the practices of purification (washing, ascetic self-denials, anointing, and so on) and of sacrifice (of food, of flowers, of money, and occasionally of the still living bodies of wives whose dead husbands rest in the flames of the funeral pyre). Sacrifice plays a central role in everyday religious practices because it is crucial in maintaining the harmony of the world as that process is conceived in the Hindu worldview. As inscribed in the sacred Vedic texts, the cosmic process requires sacrifice for renewal; through sacrifice, humans are also renewed and returned to harmony. In Hindu culture even today, the repeated daily rituals of purification and sacrifice determine both family and social time, marking the hours of the day and the schedule for the week and the month in a yearly cycle.

Given this centrality of ritual, asking how Hinduism shapes and frames gender relations invites us to ask: Which gender performs particular rituals? Through ritual, Hindus construct identity and social location, making the holy visible and tangible. No rituals are more fraught with the dangerous energy of the holy than those that surround, give shape to, and orchestrate death and burial. Practices surrounding the end of life provide a clarifying window into various religious beliefs. Our burial rituals reflect how we believe we should live. Do we believe that in death we go alone before God in final judgment, or in a cultural collectivism that calls for us to be benignly gathered to our ancestors? In either case, the myths and rituals concerning death do much to model and shape our ongoing common life.

In Hinduism, a priest or an official religious mediator does not hold central stage at death; the most important person is the oldest surviving son. As a Hindu sage and guru once told me: "You can keep your heaven if you let me have my eldest son." Given this cultural reality, I will argue later that one of the boldest and most empowering of religious innovations for Hindu women would be to construct a role for them equal to that played by the eldest son in the rituals of death. I learned this from the religious scholar who will be our principle guide in this chapter, Anantanand Rambachan. Let me introduce him.

Anant, as I will call him, was born in Trinidad, where his great-grandparents had fled to escape a famine in northern India. His family was of the elite Brahman caste *(jatis)*, and his father performed the ceremonies and conducted the religious instruction needed by the Hindu community of that Caribbean island. Yet his mother, a brilliant student, despite her caste privilege or perhaps because of it, was married when she was just twelve years old (as was the custom), ending her formal education. Her loss haunts the moral imagination of Anant because it inscribes in the tangible stuff of personal biography the whole panorama of gender relations that are acted out daily in traditional Hindu society.

In the 1970s Anant studied for his doctorate at the University of Leeds in England, where he came to know and respect a liberation theology that had taken root among Christians in his own part of the world. The consciousness-raising process brought Eurocentric thought under a subversive criticism that freed scholars from developing nations to look with new respect and hope to their own indigenous religions and cultures. It was not an easy road for Anant to follow. Examining life in modern India, he discovered that much had changed. Many families of the favored castes now choose the education of their daughters over their early marriage. Still, Anant discovered a disturbing irony at work, especially among the upwardly mobile in rural villages. Because the Brahman caste continues to enjoy high social esteem, other castes—as they climb the social ladder—have begun to take on, as a form of conspicuous display, traditional Brahman attitudes toward women. It is called *Sanskritization* and, as the word implies, describes how the newly well-to-do in rural Indian villages reenact the old Brahman habits of closeting women, denying them access to school and to learning skills for paid work outside the home. Illiteracy and obligatory child matrimony have become, yet again, badges of family honor extracted from the lives of women.

For Anant it was not an easy task to unearth the resources within his own religious practices for liberation and gender justice. However, it was a necessary task. It is also necessary for us as Western observers. It would be a mistake—and an arrogant injustice to the realities of life between men and women in modern Hindu societies—to close the case concerning Hindu gender practices on a uniformly negative note. Like other world religions, Hinduism has positive resources for addressing gender injustices and working toward the empowerment of women's lives. After all, no matter the culture or the religion, women are not and never have been passive—not in any culture, not in any time. Women have and do resist; they find spaces for dissent, places to share their stories and transform their sorrows. Women persistently teach their daughters the empowering arts of resistance and battle to insert their own narratives within the heritage of sacred texts for succeeding generations of women to read. With the help of our guide, we will look now at this other side of the picture, one that holds out promise for those Hindus who, rather than abandon their heritage of the sacred, prefer to use it to seek justice in gender relations.

Even in *The Code of Manu*, a second, different, and more promising discourse concerning women was announced:

> Women must be honored and adorned by their father, brothers, husbands, and brothers-in-law, who desire (their own) welfare.
> Where women are honored, there the gods are pleased, but where they are not honored, no sacred rite yields.
> Where the female relations live in grief, the family soon wholly perishes, but that family where they are not unhappy ever prospers.

Even here, however, the problem persists that the admonition for respect toward women remains clearly an intra-male discourse—men talking to other men *about women*. This issue of perspective and voice is evident in almost all the sacred writings we will discuss. Think of Moses or Jesus of Nazareth, think of the Prophet Muhammad or Gautama Buddha—all men mostly addressing other men. However charitable its intent, it is still male-to-male talk, with the female speaker or intended audience conspicuous in its absence. Indeed, this book takes on this same burden, but self-consciously and with the purpose of exposing and deconstructing male bias.

As with other religions, Hinduism needs what Paul Ricoeur has called "a hermeneutic of suspicion." However, criticism should be followed by "a hermeneutic of recovery." Addressing the task of recovery, Anant begins by citing a Sanskrit text that he then denounces—but denounces in the name of a more fundamental Hindu belief. He quotes from the *Ramacaritamanasa*, where Anasuya, wife of the sage Atri, instructs Sita about the duties of a respected Hindu wife.

> Listen, O princess; mother, father and brother are all friendly helpers to a limited degree; but a husband, Sita, is an unlimited blessing; and vile is the woman who refuses to serve him. Though her lord be old, sick, dull-headed, indigent, blind, deaf, bad-tempered or utterly wretched—yet if the wife treats him with disrespect, she shall suffer all the torments of hell! To be devoted in thought and word and deed to her husband's feet is her only religious duty, her only guiding rule.

Anant's comment is direct and dismissive. He argues that such religiously sanctioned patriarchal and androcentric views, embedded in sacred texts, are the major problem facing women in the Hindu tradition. He further argues that such texts are secondary in importance, even contradictory to the most fundamental beliefs of Hinduism, which have to do with the very *being* of human beings. While Hinduism holds that the divine is present in everything living, it is uniquely and most excellently displayed in the human being—in *all* human beings. The human self *(ātman)* is either identical with the divine spirit *(brahman)*, as the non-dualists believe, or a relationship of inseparability but not identity. As the *Bhagavadgītā* (13:27) holds:

> He who sees the Supreme Lord,
> Existing alike in all beings
> Not perishing when they perish,
> Truly sees.

What this implies is an encompassing vision of equality that logically should be construed also in terms of gender.

> In a Brahman endowed with wisdom and cultivation,
> In a cow, in an elephant,

And even in dog or in a dog-cooker,
The pundits see the same *(ātmān)*.
Even here on earth, rebirth is conquered
By those whose mind is established in impartiality.
Brahman is guiltless and impartial;
Therefore they are established in Brahman.

It is not only modern Hindus who can find in such a claim an original and originating sanction for gender equality. Already in the *Svetasvatara Upanisad* (circa fourth century B.C.E.) the divine is consciously identified with women *(stri)* and unmarried girls *(kumari)* as well as with men and boys.

You are a woman; you are a man; you are a boy or also a girl. As an old man, you totter along with a walking-stick. As you are born, you turn your face in all directions.
You are the dark blue bird, and the oceans. You live as one without a beginning of your pervasiveness, you from whom all beings are born.

From this passage Anant concludes that women should be understood to have value and significance in Hinduism, even as do men, because of their being, not because of their instrumental role in society as wives and mothers. They equally bear and embody the divine. Women, too, are *ātmān brahman*.

Indeed, one advantage of Hinduism compared to the Western monotheistic traditions is its celebration of a multitude of divinities, both male and female. While it is true that the Western religions have strong traditions criticizing idolatry, that critical spirit seems to have stopped short at the issue of gendering the divine. The biblical God is "Lord," "Mighty Warrior," "King of Heaven," "shepherd," or "Father." It is not enough to say that everyone knows that God transcends gender. As feminists remind us, talk—especially the talk that voices religious ritual—is not cheap. It imposes upon the mind and imagination the whole weight of daily prayers and piety: "When God is male, then males become gods."

In terms of everyday piety, Hinduism presents neither philosophical nor practical impediments to celebrating the feminine as equally endowed with the possibility of divinity. While many of the goddesses in Hindu texts are presented as subordinate, thus mirroring rather than contradicting the subordinate role of women in society, there remain awesome female goddesses like Kali. Through the ages, Kali has presented a resource for a subversive and radical reversal of culturally conditioned female self-valuing.

The popular image of God found replicated in temple statuary throughout India represents the divine as *ardhanar isvara;* it displays God as both male and female—one-half of the icon being male, embraced by and embracing the other half, which is female. As Anant reminds us, these feminine images of God in Hinduism are rich resources used by women in the past and still available for those who advocate gender equality and justice to retrieve, recover, and reinterpret.

The Hindu notion of the divine imminence and thus sacredness of all living things, especially of all humans, lays the foundation for its most fundamental ethical principal of *ahimsā* or nonviolence. So pervasive is this ethos of nonviolence that even a text like the *Ramacaritamanasa* of Tulasidasa, otherwise so imbued with misogynist prejudices, cannot avoid the implications of the ethical imperative. In his *Balakanda,* Tulasidasa affirms the divine pervasiveness and what it implies about the reverence due to all beings in these oft-recited words.

> Knowing that the whole universe, whether animate or inanimate, is pervaded by the spirit of Rama, I ever adore the feet of all with folded hands.
> Eight million four hundred thousand species of living beings, classified under four broad divisions, inhabit land, water, and the air.
> Realizing the whole world to be pervaded by Sita and Rama, I make obeisance with folded hands.

This same reverence for all beings and its implied ethic of *ahimsā* or nonviolence is echoed by the same author in his *Uttarakanda.* Rama, speaking to his brother Bharata, says: "Brother, there is no religious duty like benevolence and no sin like oppressing others. I have declared to you, dear brother, the verdict of all the Vedas and the Puranas, and the learned also know it."

Unfortunately, this admonition has remained an abstraction, a piously regarded admonition never brought down to earth where actual men and women live out their lives. Such spiritual abstractions characterize other religions besides Hinduism. There is a tendency in all religions to minimize the role that social structures play in people's lives. Later in this book, a scholar of Buddhism in Thailand will bring the same complaint against intensely pious people in his country who nevertheless condone adolescent female prostitution. Often nonviolence is thought of as a purely personal attitude and accomplishment that leaves *structural* violence—the violence embedded in and acted out by social institutions—without criticism, resistance, or reform.

This fact is so pervasive, so evenly distributed among unrelated religious traditions, that it leads one to suspect there is something about piety itself—or at least about those who organize and benefit from its practice in society—that simply passes by the obvious in a passion for the profound. Or the profound may be used unconsciously to obfuscate the obvious, turning concrete issues of evil into a discourse about the nature of evil, a discourse that finds satisfaction at the level of reflection and the cultivation of an aristocracy of soul. We will return to the issue of the aristocratic captivity of religion later.

For now, we turn to our Hindu guide and how Anant argues for a reconstruction (not an abandonment) of his own tradition. We should start by noting the distance he and we must travel to arrive at this goal. For example, consider one of the more offensive cultural practices, one that effectively causes injury to Hindu women—the dowry. Outlawed in India since 1961, the dowry remains an even more popular and widespread practice forty years later. It plays into the conspicuous consumption aspirations that increasingly possess the hearts and minds of Indian rural and urban populations. The commodification of value has taken over the world; in India, too, the value of a human person depends more and more on the pile of stuff one owns and displays to others.

Actually, Hinduism has a quite insightful diagnosis of this disease. As Anant reminds us, to live under the control of desire is to live under the control of illusion—a thirst for satisfactions that always turns unsatisfactory again in the next moment. In the Hindu diagnosis of the human problem, this is caused by ignorance *(avidyā)*. What we are ignorant of, living under the sway of desire, is that as a human self we are already full and complete (an *ātman* which is *brahman*). Conspicuous consumption is not a materialism, but a misplaced spiritual quest—to find in finite, temporal things the satisfaction and fullness that can only be grasped in liberation *(moksha)* from desire, to which we have mistakenly given spiritual power over our lives.

Combined with this ethos of conspicuous consumption, the dowry system in India is wreaking havoc with many women's lives. As Anant reminds us, today in India the bride is often viewed as a commodity; indeed, the bride becomes a means to other and more valuable commodities—like cars or scooters or refrigerators or even a less penurious wardrobe. A girl is often considered an anticipated and unwanted burden upon the resources of her family of origin. Families who can afford it use modern medicine to discover the gender of the fetus; if the pregnancy is deemed inauspicious, it is terminated (abortion is legal in India). Experts report that more than 95 percent of the abortions performed in India are to eliminate the birth of females, to ensure the birth of males.

If she survives until birth, the dowry system continues to place a Hindu woman in jeopardy throughout her life. Unscrupulous husbands and in-laws can subject her family of origin to continuing expectations even after marriage. Sometimes the pressure results in the suicide of the young bride. At other times, a young wife may be murdered so that the recent widower can reenter the dowry market. The favorite weapon is fire, which can explain away the horrendous death as a kitchen accident. Reliable estimates indicate that at least two women in New Delhi are killed in this manner each day.

A young Hindu woman has more to fear than such outlawed but culturally popular marital practices. She also finds herself surrounded by a set of religious beliefs that disvalue her even as it enhances the value of her eldest surviving brother. A Hindu doctrine that has gained a popular following in the West is transmigration of the soul and its subsequent reincarnation *(samsara)*. As Anant reminds us, upon the death of a father a set of ritual obligations are imposed upon the surviving son *(putra)* to insure a propitious passage for the recently deceased father. It is the son's privilege (denied to daughters) to offer the *pinda* (rice-ball) each year when the rites called *sraddha* are performed, rites that save the father from suffering in the afterlife. As *The Code of Manu* holds: "Because a son delivers his father from the hell called *put*, he is therefore called *put-ra* [a deliverer from *put*] for the Self-existent himself." A place of ritual centrality confers a premium on male Hindu children and adds to the already precarious hold of daughters upon the esteem and affection of their parents. (That so many daughters are so well loved and so welcomed into Hindu families says much about the power of the human heart to subvert the biases of both popular culture *and* orthodox religious teachings.)

Anant suggests two counter-discourses. The first is theological and stresses the idea of *karma,* which teaches personal responsibility for our destinies—not the life of inexorable fatalities. And responsibility requires choice, including the freedom to risk innovation in new ritual possibilities. The second is a practical recognition of the new social realities of modern India. No longer do daughters travel to distant villages to dwell with their husband's in-laws, nor do sons necessarily stay near the family hearth. With the rise of nuclear families, Anant suggests, a married daughter may be closer to home and possess an interest in the performance of family rituals. As we shall see, there is room in the way Hindus interpret religious texts to recognize and respond to such new circumstances and to legitimate the search for new ritual practices. However, this will require challenging, indeed trespassing on, the ideology of female pollution.

As in much of Western religious thought, Hinduism contains the idea that the female body becomes polluted during menstruation and childbirth. Although the discourse is seemingly concerned with female sexual fluids, it actually has to do with the politics of control. Men use their power to write religious texts to inscribe the bodies of women as dangerous, requiring surveillance. It is not different with us in the West. I remember attending the ordination in Philadelphia of the first eleven female priests of the Episcopal Church. There were four ordaining bishops. The ceremony required that the congregation be asked whether there was evidence that would invalidate the candidacy of those seeking to be priested. A conservative priest from a suburban Episcopal church jumped to his feet and said (I quote exactly): "There are not eleven more priests in the Episcopal Church today but four fewer bishops! What you have done is polluted the Church."

The notion of pollution harkens back to the idea of taboo, a religious perversion of the innocent material world, used in this case to project blame upon the victims of male fear and anger and

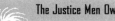

to justify the male desire to control. Anant suggests the same solution in India that we are pursuing here in the West—namely, to train women as priestesses, Hindu priestesses, fully ordained and sanctified to "handle" sacred ritual objects, as well as fully trained to write theology that is less hostile to the created being (the *ātmān-brahman*) of women.

What are the positive resources in Hindu interpretation theory that allow for innovative responses to new social circumstances both in theology and in the practices of everyday piety? Anant points out that Hinduism has traditionally distinguished between two types of sacred texts, each bearing sharply differing claims to authoritative recognition. *Sruti*, which literally means "that which is heard" (reminding us of the oral nature of the Hindu tradition), designates texts that are considered to be revelation—such as the Vedas. *Smrti*, on the other hand, means "that which is remembered" and refers to texts that are considered sacred but of human origin. The previously quoted *Code of Manu* is an example of *Smrti*. Concerning such texts, considerable interpretive freedom is allowed. Since they are understood to reflect the social and historical conditions of their origin, they can be criticized and transformed as new circumstances demand. Anant, in quoting another author affirmatively, argues that the situation of Hindu women today presents us with precisely such a case. He quotes Shashi Tharoor (*India: From Midnight to the Millennium* [New York: Arcade, 1997]):

> More attention to improving the lot of Indian women in general, empowering them to make decisions about such matters as reproduction and family expenditure, and improving their access to health care, would undoubtedly have benefited Indian society as a whole, notably by reducing the country's population. But not just that: freeing India's ordinary women from millennia of subjugation would have liberated for the country the productive talents of half the population, which for millennia have been left to languish.

The tradition provides many justifications for this task of gender liberation. The most important is found in the most fundamental of all Hindu teachings. In the *Bhagavadgītā* (18:20), the highest knowledge is "that knowledge by which one sees One imperishable being in all beings, undivided in the divided." This is contrasted to that inferior way of knowing, "which knows as separate different beings of various kinds among beings" (18:21). This undermining of a misplaced arrogance applies not simply to the distinction between species but also to invidious distinctions within the same species, as that between male and female. In humans, the female body is no less an instrument for attaining liberation *(moksa)* than the male. And this imperishable value of women is not and could not be conferred by men, because it inheres in their very *beings* and demands from men both recognition and respect.

Anant gives the case of the famous south Indian scholar and teacher, Ramana Maharshi (1879–1950), who affirmed this truth of gender equality dramatically. His own mother spent the final years of her life at his *asrama*, where she became a devoted disciple. When she died, Ramana was convinced that her devotion was such that she had attained liberation and was not subject to rebirth. It is the custom to bury the body of a liberated person rather than to cremate it; Ramana began to do just that when he was interrupted by male disciples who doubted that the body of a liberated woman should be treated with the same respect as that of a liberated man. Ramana's response was sharp and to the point: "Since *Jnana* (Knowledge) and *Mukti* (Deliverance) do not differ with the differences of sex, the body of a woman Saint also need not be burnt. Her body is also the abode of God." It is hard to conceive a more direct attack upon the ignorance *(aviate)* that displays itself in disgraceful attitudes toward the female body and its natural functions and fluids.

There is ample ancient support for the right of Hindu women to education, including scholarship in religion. The *Brhadaranyaka Upanisad* (iv. 4.18), for example, recommends to the householder a special ritual to ensure the birth of a "scholarly daughter." The early forest universities were fully coeducational; after the *upanayana* or sacred thread ceremony, girls were entitled to study the Vedas. Indeed, female students of one order were revered as the *brahmaradinis*, who committed themselves to a lifelong study of liturgical texts and are remembered as engaging in lively debates on disputed points. More recently, in the modern Indian state of Kerala, a 100 percent literacy rate has been achieved among both boys and girls—a rate far higher than that of the United States. One result of this universal education is that the birthrate in Kerala is two children per family, with a survival rate among girls equal or

superior to that of boys, which exactly reverses the trends in the rest of India as well as in most other developing countries.

Having stressed the positive resources in the Hindu sacred traditions for the work of gender justice and empowering women, I must conclude with a note of caution. While Hindu revelation or *sruti* like the Vedas and the Upanisads offer some helpful material, the prevailing ethos of the Brahman heritage remains androcentric and even misogynistic. Given the argument made above for the centrality in Hindu religious teaching that the absolute exists equally in all beings, we can say, with the famous Sankara, "A hundred *srutis* may declare that fire is cold or that it is dark; still they possess no authority in the matter." Or as Anant boldly concludes, wherever old revelation (*sruti*) that demeans women is found, it must be replaced by new revelation that asserts the full equality and rights of women and obliges Hindu men to join with Hindu women in the mutual struggle for justice in gender relations.

2. Christianity

THE EARLY CHRISTIAN CHURCH WAS NOT what the earliest followers of Jesus had in mind. The rise of the church was, instead, the
result of two wholly unexpected crises. The first was the crisis of the
delayed parousia—that eagerly anticipated return of the heavenly
Christ. His establishment of the kingdom of God was first expected
at any moment, then put on temporary hold, and eventually put on
indefinite hold. Jesus' followers had to settle down and live in this
world for a while. They needed to think about the world in a sys-
tematic way—produce a worldview—and develop a set of instructions for everyday life—construct an ethos. To complicate the task,
the early followers of Jesus had to face a second crisis—their world
was not Jewish but Greco-Roman. The New Testament was written not in Hebrew but in Greek.

In response to this double crisis, the early church developed its
institutions, its liturgies, its fundamental theology, and (along with
other moral prescriptions) its concept of the proper relations
between women and men. We should note that the church developed in communities that were at first mostly cut off from power
and social prestige, communities that represented themselves to
potential converts as transcending the invidious distinctions of
their society. For example, Saint Paul wrote to his fellow Christians
reminding them that in Christ "there is neither slave nor free, there
is neither male nor female" (Gal 3:28). This statement of fundamental equality should be balanced, however, by the recognition
that these same Christian communities became convinced that the
most excellent way of being "in Christ" was the celibate life.

The body came to be viewed as problematic by the early church
because it was viewed as problematic in the Greco-Roman world
where the church was establishing its residence. Among the intellectual elite, the nature and destiny of the material realm was
viewed with profound pessimism. Responding to this, a popular,

second-century Christian named Marcion spoke for many in denying the created goodness not just of the human body but also of the
whole of material existence. He presented a cosmic dualism that
divided spirit against matter. That dualism remained influential
two centuries later in the writings of a Persian teacher by the name
of Mani, writings that would speak deeply to the confusions,
heartache, and search for order of a young man whom we would
later know as Saint Augustine.

The church would eventually condemn Marcion as a heretic, but
the appeal of his pessimism ran deep. Marcion viewed human liberation as escape from the seductions and illusions of the material
world and ascent and mystical union with the God of pure spirit
or light. Key to this escape was a special knowledge (*gnosis* in
Greek) allegedly left by Christ as a secret gospel. For those persuaded to flee this material world, sexuality—by which the human
body (thought of as a prison and a tomb) was reproduced—was
viewed with fear and contempt. And responsibility for this cata-
strophe was thought to belong in a special way to women. Had not
Eve seduced Adam and with that single bite of the apple brought
sin and death upon us all? Among these Christian Gnostics, the
sons of Adam—not the daughters of Eve—could hope for salvation. Thus we find a collection of 114 secret sayings allegedly left
by Jesus in the Gospel of Thomas, including the following
exchange: "[The disciple] Simon Peter said to them, 'Let Mary
leave us, for women are not worthy of life.' Jesus said, 'I myself
shall lead her in order to make her male, so that she too may
become a living spirit resembling you males. For every woman who
will make herself male will enter the kingdom of heaven'"(114).

The church would reject such misogynistic attitudes as well as
the wider cosmic dualism of spirit and body. Instead, the material
world, together with the human body, would be affirmed as part of
God's good creation. Still, the suspicion of sexuality and its pas-
sions and of women as temptresses of men would linger, partially
because of the picture of the larger cosmic order that the church
borrowed from Neoplatonism. It was a worldview put together in
terms of an up-and-down chain of being, ranked from the fullness
of being, God, at the top down to the lowest degree of being, matter, at the bottom. Love for the divine fullness was the animating

principle of the whole, while love turned down and fixing its long-
ing upon anything less than the divine produced that disordered
love *(dillectio inordinata)* called sin.

How the early church came to terms with life in this world, and
with men and women and sexuality as part of that life, is summa-
rized in the thought of the most influential voice in the whole of
Western Christianity, Saint Augustine of Hippo (d. 430). Augustine
is quoted by Saint Thomas Aquinas and by the Protestant reformers Luther and Calvin more often than any other source except the
Bible. After a brief flirtation with the dualism of Mani, which
appealed to him because it seemed to offer insight into the tragedy
of evil, Augustine became converted to Christianity. Here too was a
powerful vision of evil—not the result of a perverse body, however,
but of a spirit that seeks to find in material satisfactions what is
available only in the love of God. These two loves ("the love of this
earth which despises God" or "the love of God which despises this
earth") form the battleground for Augustine's Christian journey.

While not quite adhering to a mind/body dualism, Augustine
and those who found his theology persuasive found something
about the body, especially in its sexual functioning, that remained
dangerous to the spiritual quest. That something was lust—Augustine called it concupiscence. In the proper relation of the two genders, rightly ordered love *(dillectio ordinata)* directs the love of
each gender first toward God and secondarily, and only in that love
as ordered by God, toward one another. Therefore, the divinely
ordained purpose of sexuality was not pleasure or companionship
but reproduction. Augustine believed that this hierarchal and prop-
erly ordered love was temporarily suspended in the heat of sexual
intercourse. And it was by way of this act that original sin was
transmitted from one generation to the next. This end-oriented
teleological ethic (borrowed from Roman Stoicism), combined
with the continuing suspicion of sexual pleasure cut loose from the
conscious and rational intention of reproduction, determines to
this day the negative position many Christians hold on contraception and family planning.

Thus, what had started out five centuries earlier as a community in which the distinction between slave and free or male and
female disappeared in the unity of Christ had become a community

hierarchically organized under the domination of a male priest-hood that had fled intimate contact with women. The church had come to terms with life in this world and with the lives of the men and women living within it through a worldview and an ethos that silenced the voice of women in churches where once they had prophesied and preached. The church delegated to its celibate male priesthood the sole right to handle the sacred elements of the Eucharist, to hear confession, to grant absolution, to baptize, to marry, and to anoint the sick and the dying. The first letter addressed to Timothy, which was not written by Saint Paul but was accepted by the early church as an authentic expression of apos-tolic instruction, summarizes all too plainly this sad story: "A woman must receive instruction silently and under complete con-trol. I do not permit a woman to teach or to have authority over a man. She must be quiet. For Adam was formed first, then Eve. Fur-ther, Adam was not deceived but the woman was deceived and transgressed" (1 Tim 2:11-14).

But if that were the only legacy left from those days, this chapter would never have been written. In turning to the positive resources in Christianity for gender justice and the empowerment of women, I need to recognize our principle guides—the Roman Catholic bib-lical scholar Father Gerard Sloyan and the Protestant social ethicist Marvin Ellison.

Sloyan begins his story with Jesus of Nazareth and the women who were his more or less constant companions. While there is rea-son to doubt the authenticity of some of the teachings, parables, and miracles of Jesus in the New Testament—which were instead manufactured by the early church—there is no reason to doubt the general picture the Gospels give us of his daily life as an itinerant preacher and healer and the easy companionship he enjoyed with women. Given the expectations of first-century Semitic culture, it is remarkable that Jesus is presented to us as unmarried. However, John the Baptist is similarly remembered. Perhaps both were too busy with their missions and were convinced that the messianic age was imminent.

Sloyan points out that the various Gospels report that "many women" accompanied Jesus in his travels and supported his small band financially out of their private means. Jesus is also remem-bered as welcoming women who for various reasons were shunned by the polite society of his time and as perhaps even saving the life of one who was threatened with stoning. Contrary to Jewish convention, he engaged in a lengthy debate with a Samaritan woman at Jacob's well, making a dramatic and even revolutionary statement that outcast ethnic groups would be welcomed into his company. How deeply he engaged the loyalty of women and was rewarded in turn with their steadfast courage in danger is recorded in the memory of his final hours, when his mother and two other women stayed by him at his execution, long after his male followers had fled and abandoned him.

Sloyan draws our attention to the hard line Jesus of Nazareth took on the matter of divorce as an example of his boldness in defense of women. It was both custom and law at the time that a husband could divorce his wife to marry a second by simply proclaiming three times in a public place, "I divorce you!" While the early church would develop many laws and practices concerning a second marriage while the first wife still lived, it followed the example of Jesus in never sanctioning the otherwise common patriarchal privilege of dismissing one wife to marry another. In those days, a woman thus repudiated entered a precarious, indeed even perilous, social condition.

Jesus showed himself not simply to be at ease with women, enjoying their friendship, but siding with them against established practices that threatened their well-being. Nonetheless, as Sloyan reminds us, in most matters of gender the Jesus of the Gospels is presented as a Jew amongst Jews, a man of first-century Semitic culture, who neither presumed nor advocated the leadership or even full equality of women in family or in public life.

Turning beyond the biblical memory of Jesus of Nazareth, which is the only memory we have of him, and setting aside for the moment the suspicion of women in the early church, those looking for models of strong Christian women exercising influence and even leadership in early Christian congregations will find their task easy. We know, for example, from patristic and medieval sermons what a favorite topic Eve as temptress was. But we also know from that same literature that a piety developed concerning the virgin Mary who was conceived as Eve's alter ego—the "God-bearer" as the Council of Ephesus (431 C.E.) called her. Some see in this elevation of Mary a masculine ruse to present to women the ideal of lowliness before and obedience to males. However, a more likely motive was the desire to have Mary as a friendly advocate before her son, who was depicted in sermons and in art as ever more distant and judgmental.

Of more practical benefit to women than the veneration of Mary was the rise, in the late second century, of the right of women to remain virginal and to enter into a "religious life." The cultural practice in the patriarchal societies of the time was for fathers to arrange marriages, often for the purposes of acquiring property and rarely in response to the romantic interests of the daughter. Such marriages were often bereft of affection and descended more than occasionally into outright abuse. Knowing this, women fought for an adult life under their own control and opted for being espoused to Christ. Macrina, the sister of Basil of Caesarea and Gregory of Nyssa, founded a community of nuns in the mid-fourth century. A century-and-a-half later Scholastica, sister of Benedict, did the same. At first, the candidates came from families of wealth, but once established, the communities of religious women welcomed those too poor to possess a dowry. Here was an expanding community of committed women, self-governed under an abbess of their own choosing and treated with protection and respect by the wider community. It was a practice of self-liberation fought for and won by women. (It will be advocated in a later chapter that Buddhist women living in contemporary Thailand, especially poor women, need this same option of becoming nuns.)

There is also the memory of women who, having been denied their voice in public worship, gave witness to their courage and devotion through martyrdom. There was Blandina, martyred under Marcus Aurelius in 177 or 178, whose body was mangled beyond recognition by her torturers; before she died she could still say, "I am a Christian. We do nothing to be ashamed of!" Or there was the well-born Perpetua of Carthage, the mother of an infant son, who was martyred together with her slave Felicitas, who gave birth to an infant daughter just before her death in the arena. In a modern Catholic mass, the list of martyrs includes many men, plus Agnes, Cecilia, and Felicitas—models of women who risked death to serve God and their fellow human beings (think of the nuns working for the liberation of the poor and killed because of it in El Salvador).

Christianity also has a rich tradition of women mystics, schol-ars, and authors. As early as the mid-fourth century, Saint Marcina the Younger probably wrote a rule for nuns living on her family estate, but we do not have a copy. We do have writings of some women mystics, including Saint Gertrude of Helfta (d. c. 1302), Mechtild of Magdeburg (d. c. 1282), and Catherine of Siena (d. 1380), who made her vows as a member of the Dominican third order and who traveled with a group of peacemaking activists that included clerics. Great Britain finds its advocate in an anonymous anchoress (d. after 1416) who lived in a cell at the church of Saint Julian in Norwich and left a chronicle of her visions, published as *Showings,* that was soon to become and remains today enormously influential. Saint Bridget of Brigitta, Sweden (d. 1373), foundress of a double monastery at Vadstena, was another influential Chris-tian woman; her daughter Saint Catherine (d. 1381) followed her as the monastery's first abbess.

These women were not walled up in cloisters; while active in wor-ship, they also provided health care for other women and for the poor and offered education not only in the practical arts but also in scholarship and writing. Father Sloyan remembers with gratitude how the church in New York City educated him and two of his sis-ters to the doctoral level; one of his sisters became the president of a college and a professor of mathematics. As a Protestant, it is my con-viction that in rejecting the vocation of nuns and "women religious," the Reformation closed the door on a powerful option for women's self-empowerment. (The Anglican church is the one exception.)

These illustrious women offer modern feminists (female or male) models of liberation, of courage, of dedication, and of self-less service to others. Yes, they also occasionally model exemplary dying, from which we may profit in an age that seems so absent of models for adult women, except those dedicated to the conventions of marriage and motherhood or to the trivialization of women as presented in television and advertising.

I turn next to the insights of another friend and colleague, the Protestant ethicist Marvin Ellison. Writing as a gay man, Marvin brings the perspective of one who, early in life, experienced sexual-ity as an arena of oppression and of haunting silences and abuse. Although he grew up in the 1950s in the South as a white male of relative class privilege and received an elite education, because of his sexual orientation Marvin was, nevertheless, denied the privileges and power of patriarchy that would otherwise have been the automatic inheritance of one belonging to his race, class, and gender. Marginalized by his increasing awareness and willingness to admit his own "difference," Marvin notes that from an early age he was nurtured by a religiously rooted passion for justice. In this respect, he responded in much the same way to suffering as another scholar who will guide us later, the Muslim Farid Esack. Abandoned by his father as an infant, Farid and his four brothers had to survive on the factory paycheck of their mother under the rigors of South African apartheid, where they were not only desperately poor but also "coloured." As with Marvin, Farid responded to the evident unfairness of life with the conviction that, "for God to be God, God had to be just and on the side of the marginalized." Perhaps the similarity of the two responses should be expected. Ellison cites bell hooks, an African American social critic and writer, who argues that besides deprivation, marginality provides a place of opportunity—a perspective from which to practice freedom and to gain moral vision. Why? Because power in society includes the power to define and to name reality, and that means the price that power often pays for its privilege is a self-inflicted blindness to the realities of injustice. Viewing society from the margins, whether by force or by choice, provides a perspective of criticism to *see through* (rather than to look through) the ruling images of deservedness, which always include the image of authorized masculinity.

Power in our North American society mostly belongs to Protestant white (straight) males of class privilege. Other males have power, of course, but no Jew and only one Roman Catholic (who was then killed) has been elected president of this country. The image of obligatory masculinity in our society is largely a Protestant construction. In his insightful study *The Protestant Ethic and the Spirit of Capitalism,* Max Weber argued that at the heart of the Protestant ethos is an "inner worldly asceticism" that combines with a strong emphasis upon individualism and yields an anxious preoccupation with control—not only the control of the self but the control of others who 'might contaminate that control. Discipline, energized by an emotional coolness and rational distance, mediates a life that is systematically ordered and orderly.

If this claim about the Protestant influence upon images of social reputability and respect sounds far-fetched, consider the most successful image in the history of advertising in our society. It is the Marlboro man who never smiles, never is seen in the company of women, rides his horse, wields his lasso, and takes charge (of whom? of what?). The advertisement works because it is a false presentation of the real possibilities of most males (and of almost all females) and leaves, therefore, a surplus of self-suspicion that can be bonded with the product being sold—a cigarette. But the image of the self-possessed and powerful loner (John Wayne? Clint Eastwood? Bruce Willis?) who rides into town, cleans things up, and then rides off alone into the sunset is not just a sad picture of masculinity; it is a dangerous one. It is also disturbingly close to the image of the pilgrim presented in the once wildly popular Protestant tract, *Pilgrim's Progress.*

Marvin Ellison points out that it is no accident that the newly energized (and usually Protestant) religious right focuses its attention and draws its energy from masculine anxiety over control—in the church, in the home, in the world, and in the bedroom. Marvin argues that it is time we men start telling the truth—not for the sake of women so much as for our own sake—about how our lives have been constructed on the basis not of reciprocity and mutual respect but on the basis of competition and fear. The Marlboro man is dangerous both to others and to himself. He inflicts on himself the impossible and forever anxious and lonely task of "taking charge" and "being in control." Always failing that demand, he will always need something—a "broad," a "faggot"—to despise and feel superior to. As he ages, his own body will betray him, delivering him over finally to that ultimate "out-of-control" state, death. He will never feel safe. He will never feel sure. He will always search for what he cannot find, sometimes blame himself, but mostly blame others for it.

Martin Luther once remarked, "What your heart clings to and relies upon—that is your god." It is time to redo—both men and women together—what the Roman Catholic moral theologian Dan Maguire calls "this pelvic theology." Timely indeed, given what this masculine ideology is causing us to inflict upon the larger material (from the Latin *mater* or "mother") world of which we are a part.

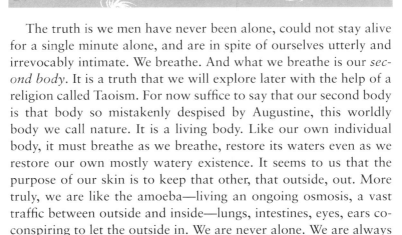

The truth is we men have never been alone, could not stay alive for a single minute alone, and are in spite of ourselves utterly and irrevocably intimate. We breathe. And what we breathe is our *second body*. It is a truth that we will explore later with the help of a religion called Taoism. For now suffice to say that our second body is that body so mistakenly despised by Augustine, this worldly body we call nature. It is a living body. Like our own individual body, it must breathe as we breathe, restore its waters even as we restore our own mostly watery existence. It seems to us that the purpose of our skin is to keep that other, that outside, out. More truly, we are like the amoeba—living an ongoing osmosis, a vast traffic between outside and inside—lungs, intestines, eyes, ears co-conspiring to let the outside in. We are never alone. We are always embraced. And when we ride toward the sunset we do not and could not possibly ride alone.

I quote again from Martin Luther, who got close to the truth when he said: "It is not only heaven that is pure, with its stars, where Christ reigns in his work; but earth too is clean, with its trees and its grass, where we are at home with all that is ours." We humans, and all other living things here on Earth, are blessed by a gloriously contaminated intimacy in and with this world. Inheritors of Augustine, we Christians, both Catholic and Protestant, need to work on a theology of creation that is less angry, less arrogant, more grateful, and more accurate. Pilgrims who have lost our way, we must reconceive where we belong and to whom and what we belong.

Some of these legacies from the Christian past are helpful in the search for gender justice; some of them are burdens that must be cast off and left behind. But what are the resources and strategies Christians of the industrialized world can use in seeking the empowerment of the marginalized—the poor, mostly women and their children—while respecting the natural environment upon which all of us remain utterly dependent?

One of the most important resources Christianity possesses is its geographic distribution across the world (Islam is similarly widespread). As an institution of authority and loyalty both within but also beyond another institution of authority and loyalty—the state—the worldwide church offers the possibility of hearing the voices of women in developing countries—the poorest of the poor—in a solidarity that transcends national boundaries. We who have money because we benefit from our senior membership in the global capitalism that now dominates the world have a special responsibility. For the first time in all of human history, the poor of the world need money. Previously, day-by-day subsistence and survival was "in the hands" of the poor themselves. They could grow or gather food, sew garments, and build shelter out of indigenous natural materials. But not any more! The global market has drawn the everyday life of all of us, the poor included, into a worldwide monetary system. According to the present rules of the game, money knows only one loyalty—and that is to make more money. The poor of the world chase after money because food costs money, clothing costs money, even clean water costs money! So they leave the villages where there is no paid work and move to the city. It is the largest migration in recorded human history, and it is happening right now. Money—not just big money but the money made by children selling water bottles and cigarettes to motorists caught on jammed city streets—has woven itself as never before into the intimacies of everyday survival. What the International Monetary Fund admits was a "slight miscalculation" in restructuring the economy of Indonesia after the Asian monetary crisis in 1997 resulted in the tripling—in one year—of the infant mortality rate in the fourth largest country of the world.

What are Christians in prosperous countries, in conversation with Christians and others in developing countries, going to do about money? How and why and where should money move? Who will eat and who will starve? As Protestant ethicist Larry Rasmussen reminds us, Christianity is reinventing itself globally "from [being] the religion of the rich to [becoming a] faith of the poor." Christians of the older churches will need to learn how to listen to the thunder of that future. As Rasmussen says, "the vitality of Christian faith has passed from the European and North American world to peoples in Africa, Latin America, and Asia, to the women's movement most everywhere, and to communities in our own midst who are most in touch with these."

We have the money. We have the armies. Around the world people who begin to acquire money want to own what we already own, what we started owning long ago. We should remind ourselves that the Hebrew prophets, whom Jews, Christians, and Muslims share,

were convinced that God (and therefore the long arm of history) measures nations and their interactions not from the top down but from the bottom up.

We have a resource that will help us get in touch with that notion. Latin American liberation theology reminds us that there are two kinds of violence—horizontal and vertical. Horizontal violence is what we see on our nightly television news, the violence that victims of unjust power inflict upon other victims. It is the violence we who are usually not its victims deplore and whose perpetrators we put in jail. Vertical or structural violence is the violence done by oppressive institutions, the violence that wears uniforms, the violence done with quiet decorum in the executive boardroom. It is far more effective than horizontal violence because people do not call it violence but just "the way things are." An important gift given to Christians of the industrialized world is the companionship of Christians from other countries, who join with us in the struggle for justice and allow us to cross borders and see the world from the bottom up, a perspective that can give sight to the blind.

For poor women especially, family planning, including a woman's choice for abortion, is crucial in their always-fragile search for control over their own lives. As Marvin Ellison points out, birth by choice is always preferable to birth by coercion or necessity and is a good that enhances the well-being of women and thus the well-being of us all. The right to choose abortion obviously includes the right to choose against abortion or against forced sterilization. Women's bodies are put under attack in different ways in different cultures. For example, an obvious thing we men owe women is not to give them an unwanted pregnancy or disease. This requires of us males a new sense of responsibility for our sexual practices, a rewriting of the predatory masculinity still written into our television and movie scripts that brag about sexual intimacy as a "score" or "getting laid."

Another positive resource found in Christian history and practice is its graphic and public acting out of alternative and even subversive models of male and female sexual roles—men without children or significant bank accounts choosing to serve meals to others at mass; women choosing to live in communities of their own kind and under their own rule. Clearly, these need to be choices—not rules imposed from above—if they are to have significant cultural impact as true alternatives. But they remain significant dramas of difference just the same. In another drama of difference, many Christian churches already baptize the children of gay and lesbian couples, while some (though not many) are beginning to sanctify such interpersonal unions.

We should also remember Christianity's heroic forebears, both men and women, "heroic" because they struggled for justice against unjust power—Harriet Tubman, Archbishop Romero, Elizabeth Cady Stanton, Dietrich Bonhoeffer, the list could go on and on. These stories of saints and martyrs offer powerful alternatives for the young who are searching to find a meaningful adult identity while traveling through the wasteland of a culture grown morally flabby with conspicuous consumption and increasing inequality. Such memories of heroes also present the opportunity to those of us who are not young to think about how we want to be remembered and judged. In this alternative approach, we are encouraged to give up our misplaced attachment to the culturally popular values and valuables that we use to keep our fragile identities in focus—values that, when we think they determine our worth as persons, end up stealing us from ourselves.

We began our examination of Christianity and gender justice with the unexpected journey that the early Jesus movement took as it left Jerusalem behind and found its future in a Greco-Roman culture that had significant suspicions about the human body, which it associated with disease and death. One of the leaders left behind in Jerusalem was James, who in *Letter of James* wrote to fellow Christians about what constitutes "pure religion." It is, the author thought, something both simple and difficult. It is "visiting the widows and orphans in their distress." What widows and orphans have in common are the precarious circumstances of their survival. That is precisely what Christianity teaches us concerning men's obligations to women. It teaches us men to identify fully and gratefully with the human condition, with what is exposed and precarious—with our body that gives us life, with women who give us our body, and with the material earth that every day nourishes and supports us all.

3. Islam

SOME PRELIMINARY REFLECTIONS WILL HELP US get our discussion started. When we in the West who are not Muslims begin to think about Islam and gender, we are likely to have a biased picture in our minds. Thanks to television, we envision Muslim women dressed in black robes that cover them from head to ankle. What we think is that these women are forced to live under Islamic patriarchy. But all dress is a cultural uniform—ours as much as anyone's. And *seeing is political*. What does that mean?

When we see bodies we do not see light waves. We see meanings projected upon those bodies, meanings that allow us to recognize what we see. We see bodies, for example, that are male or female, tall or short, old or young, fat or thin, black or white, brown or yellow. The words we attach to bodies have no natural meaning. They are social constructs that reflect how power works in society; they reinforce how power works. The politics of seeing is so effective because it disguises itself as *the not seen* in what we see.

In our society a young, tall, and thin woman is generally seen as desirable. However, a thin woman in North Africa or South Asia is not considered desirable because in those cultures her thinness signifies the poverty of her family and means she will not bring a good bride-price. So, what is it that we Westerners see when we see Muslim women dressed in clothing that covers them from head to feet? We see a uniform strikingly different from those worn by women in our own society, where female uniforms are designed to disclose bodies, to let those bodies be seen in full flesh and contour. Which uniform displays liberation from patriarchy? To answer the question, we must ask who has power and how does power work in the seeing and in the being seen. Is it the one who is being seen who has power, or does the one seeing have power? Uniforms, ours as well as others', require critical reflection, reflection on the *politics of seeing*.

As there is a politics of seeing, so also there is a *politics of knowing*. We talk today about "Islam and the West." But Islam as a category of understanding was invented by Western scholars who invented the West in the same process. It was a colonial construction of the late nineteenth century that named one part of the world "modern," "developed," "first" and at the same time named the other world "traditional" and in need of modernization and development (in other words, of becoming like the West). Like seeing, the production, certification, and distribution of knowledge are political. Knowledge is an expression and instrument of power. That is why in this chapter I shall depend on two Muslim guides in an admittedly fundamental way. We will observe Islam through Islamic eyes, and in doing so enter more deeply into the critical task.

Our guides will be Asghar Ali Engineer from India and Farid Esack from South Africa. Both agree that any discussion of Islam and gender must begin with an analysis of the *Qur'an,* the holy scriptures of Islam. Although they begin at the same place and argue from a pro-feminist position, they read the *Qur'an* in strikingly different ways. One uses the *Qur'an* on behalf of the rights and the dignity of women against all the rest of the various authoritative sources Islam has traditionally recognized, which Asghar sees as socially and historically situated and tainted by patriarchy. But Farid subjects the Qur'anic text itself to criticism as he interrogates it on issues of gender and justice.

Both agree that Islam thinks of itself as portraying a total way of life—a construction or model of correct religious beliefs and ritual practices but also of values, customs, and laws to shape the whole of everyday life. All of this is thought to have begun with the *Qur'an* and the Prophet Muhammad to whom, most Muslims believe, God directly dictated his revelation through the angel Gabriel. And for the majority of Muslims it is not just the *Qur'an* that is authoritative; the words of commentary on that revelation by the prophet as recorded by his companions and the way of life he displayed in word and deed (the *ahadith* or *Sunna*) are thought to present an exemplary model. Both Engineer and Esack enter reservations concerning that traditional notion of authoritative instruction and do so in the name of gender justice. Both claim that in doing that they display a continuing deep attachment and loyalty to Islam.

Asghar and Farid bring the same accusations and complaints about the treatment of women in traditional Islam. They criticize the right legitimated by Islamic law *(Shari'ah)* of multiple marriages (up to four) for men and their right to marry Jews or Christians, rights denied Muslim women. Both criticize the practice of obligatory female veiling (the *hijab*) and the notion behind it that blames women and their bodies for excessive male sexual excitement. This notion that women and their sexuality require strict male supervision and control is behind today's practice in conservative Muslim societies of confining women to the household. Concerning male sexual conduct, both Asghar and Farid deplore the legitimization in the past of free sexual access to female slaves.

On the other hand, both our guides point to the fact that in the early period in Mecca both genders occupied the same space at worship in the mosque, and women could interpret the law—an equality that was quickly lost in succeeding generations as women were not only segregated in worship, but excluded from religious leadership. This practice was extended into civil society where women were excluded from the study of the law *(Shari'ah)*, thus from an active role in *shura* (consultation) and *ijma* (the forming of consensus). The exclusion of the female voice is, in fact, the central complaint both Asghar and Farid bring against their own tradition (as it is others' central complaint against Hinduism and Christianity). Not only are female voices excluded from the authoritative texts; the texts are clearly written to a male audience. They are discourses by men to other men *about* women. The *Qur'an* is not excluded from this complaint.

Both argue that, generally speaking, the *Qur'an* is strong in defense of the weak and calls for justice for the marginalized; these attitudes are supported by the concrete actions of the prophet. The established practices of pre-Islamic Arabia assigned women to a clearly inferior social position and reduced them as a gender to the marginalized. Against this, the *Qur'an* admonishes: "Muslim men and women, believing men and women, obedient men and women . . . for them God had prepared forgiveness and a handsome reward" (Q. 23:35). And, "Whosoever does good deeds, whether male or female and he [or she] they shall enter the garden and shall not be dealt with unjustly" (Q. 219). Or, "They [women] have rights similar to those against them" (Q. 2:228).

And, "To men a share of what their parents and kinsmen leave and to women a share of what parents and relatives leave" (Q. 4.7). And, "To the adulteress and the adulterer, whip each one of them a hundred lashes . . . " (Q. 24.2). Pro-feminist Islamic scholars use these verses (and many others could be cited) to argue the case that the *Qur'an* favors gender justice. This is Asghar's position. But Farid points out that in most of these verses, the interpretation is key—and it is a key that is left to the male voice. In the case of women's rights, the operative word is "similar" and leaves open how that is to be determined. As to inheritance, the key word is "share"—again left open to (male) interpretation that, as a matter of law, decided that daughters were to get half the share that sons get. As to adultery, it is a male interpretation that decides who is or is not an adulterer. Pregnancy of an unmarried woman is automatic proof of adultery, while the naming of the male partner in such a case, in absence of witnesses to the act, is in the eyes of law tantamount to slander.

Both authors find the Qur'anic teaching on wife beating highly problematic. The central text reads as follows:

> Men are *qawwamun* (the Protectors and maintainers) of/over *'ala* (women), because God has *faddala* (preferred) some of them over others, and because they support them from their means.
>
> Therefore the *salihat* (righteous) women are *qanitat* (devoutly obedient), and guard in their husband's absence what God would have them guard.
>
> As to those women on whose part you fear *nushuz* (ill-conduct/disobedience), admonish them, refuse to share their beds and beat them. But if they return to obedience seek not means against them.
>
> For God is the most high, Great above you. (Q. 4:34)

Even Asghar, who wants to use the *Qur'an* as a weapon of authority on behalf of gender justice, bridles at this instruction. He admits that even the *Qur'an* sometimes speaks in a culturally specific way and voice. He points out that the prophet himself, while personally inclined to support equal retaliation of a wife against a husband, when faced with strong objection by Arab males had his opinion overruled by subsequent revelation. The prophet is reported to have said: "We [himself] wanted something and God wanted something else, and what God wants is best." Asghar wonders just what it was in this case that the prophet was submitting to.

Farid argues even more fundamentally. He points out that while the *Qur'an* often speaks charitably about women—"the best of you is he who behaves best with his wives. . . . Listen, treat women well!" (Q. 2:118), the problem is that it is a male voice talking to a male audience about how *they* (men) should or should not treat *them* (women). The actors and the ones to be acted upon are gender specific; the *Qur'an* displays gender bias regarding those addressed and instructed and those not addressed and not instructed—those excluded from the discourse. Moreover, for the vast majority of Muslims, the *Qur'an* is viewed as "eternal and uncreated," the veritable "speech of God" transmitted without error by the prophet. For Farid such a notion is highly dubious for any Muslim dedicated to gender justice. How can one be content, he asks, with a Transcendent One who speaks about you (as a woman) but hardly ever to you? And how can men intent upon the rights and dignity of women be content?

Farid concludes that one is driven by the call to justice and compassion to admit the male-biased context not simply *of* the Qur'anic text (its hearers) but *within* the text itself (its voice). Once one admits to that radical contextualization, the door swings open to fundamental reinterpretation of the sacred heritage for the purposes of pursuing gender justice. Farid insists that such a reinterpretation displays an honest and therefore true veneration of the textual legacy. To those who accuse him of violating the text of the *Qur'an*, Farid replies without a blink. If forced to choose between violence toward the text and textual legitimization of violence against real people, he gladly pleads guilty to the former. Accused by a Muslim pro-feminist scholar and a woman of no longer being a Muslim, Farid replied: "Am I seriously to believe that on the Day of Final Judgment God will ask me, 'How did you deal with My Text?'"

What Farid does to the *Qur'an*, Asghar is much more comfortable doing to the rest of the texts held sacred by most Muslims. He puts into their social and historical context the prophet's sayings, the prophet's remembered actions, and the whole process by which

Islamic law (*Shari'ah*) was established and written down. Where *shura* (consultation) is absent the voice of women, there *ijma* (consensus) is not valid. The entire legal tradition is thereby opened for reexamination and reinterpretation. Asghar's publicly stated position has nearly cost him his life.

Born into an intensely religious home, from an early age Asghar studied not only the *Qur'an* and *tafsir* (commentary), but also *ahadith* (the prophet's sayings) and Islamic law and theology. He finds himself as an adult so feared and hated by the conservative but politically powerful Bohar Muslim priesthood in India that he suffered beatings and attempted assassinations five times. Mild-mannered and less radical in his scholarship than his friend Farid Esack, his life is at risk because he dares to criticize the rigid traditionalism and literalism that are the expression of piety required as proof of loyalty by many of his fellow Muslims.

Both Farid and Asghar agree that what we are confronted with in the *Qur'an*, given a few notable exceptions, is a formidable liberation theology and ethic. This theology completely integrates piety and worship with the practices of justice in the intimate details of everyday life. However, the *Qur'an* is far more detailed in its theology than in its ethical prescriptions. This left the door necessarily open to subsequent interpretation, where the male chauvinism of the surrounding Arab culture found entrance. Still, the original intent remains clear. Justice is more than fairness, more than procedural correctness, more than honest contracts. Justice is the active defense of the poor and the weak and enjoins all believers in the task of liberation from all that degrades and denies human dignity and worth. The *Qur'an* even hints at a necessary revolution *from below.* "And We desire to bestow a favour upon those who were deemed weak in the land, and to make them the leaders, and to make them the heirs" (Q. 28:5).

Anyone who has spent time living in a Muslim country as I have, and living there as a guest and stranger, can bear witness to the elaborate generosity, seemingly bordering on the foolhardy, that is displayed toward the stranger, the visitor, the other. In Islam, justice requires more than being nice: It requires sacrifice. Justice is measured by the needs of the weak and the marginal, not by the generosity or easy resources of the powerful and well off. The

Qur'an uses the treatment of women and children who are in danger and unable to care for themselves ("widows and orphans") as the most trustworthy measure. Armed with that authorization, Asghar takes on patriarchal arrogance wherever he finds it in his tradition.

He focuses his critique upon the body of Islamic law called *Shari'ah*, held by most Muslims to be divine and thus immutable. Quite the contrary, Asghar claims. *Shari'ah* was collected and codified under thoroughly specific historical and cultural circumstances—namely, the patriarchal bias of the Arab culture within which early Islam took root. For example, the prophet explicitly forbade the collecting of his own sayings because he (quite correctly) anticipated they would be mistakenly venerated and granted a spurious authority. Nevertheless, the collection of the *Sunna* (or *ahadith*) was made and became—as the prophet feared—a foundation stone, equally valid with the *Qur'an*, in the formulation of *Shari'ah*. It is precisely in this *Shari'ah*, codified in the second and third centuries after the prophet's death, that one finds enshrined the restrictive codes—on female dress, on access to education and civil society. It also contains restrictions on the role of women in public worship as well as various provisions concerning divorce, custody of children, maintenance, and inheritance that sharply privilege the male position.

All of this runs precisely opposite to the word and spirit of the *Qur'an*, Asghar claims. He points to a practice widespread among Arabs of that time called *zihar*—men declaring their wives to be "like the back of their mothers" and summarily abandoning them. Against this popular practice the *Qur'an* spoke out boldly: "Those of you who put away their wives by calling them their mothers—they are not their mothers. None are their mothers save those who give them birth, and they utter indeed a hateful word and lie . . . " (Q. 58:2). Even more contemptuous is the Qur'anic condemnation of the cultural bias of that time of so preferring the birth of a son to that of a daughter that fathers, faced with the perceived dishonor of a daughter's birth, would sometimes bury their female children alive. "When news is brought to one of them of a female child, his face darkens and he is filled with inward grief. With shame does he hide himself from his people because of the bad news he received. Shall he retain her in contempt or bury her in the dust? Ah what evil choice they decide on!" (Q. 16:58-59).

That is a powerful, countercultural response. And Asghar argues that, in condemning local customs that assaulted the well-being of women, the *Qur'an* establishes itself as a text that stands in opposition to and against the patriarchal practices then common to the larger society. But sadly, this voice of liberation was lost as generations of *ulama* (male legal experts) turned increasingly to the collected sayings of the prophet (many of them of doubtful origin) and to local customary law *('adat)* and in so doing enshrined male domination and even misogyny under the mantle of divine legislation *(Shari'ah)*.

Against what has now become a rigid traditionalism, Asghar holds out the ancient option of *ijtihad*—using reason to address new problems. It is a matter under hot debate in Islamic societies today, with conservative clerics arguing that the gates of *ijtihad* have long been closed. Against that position, Asghar quotes the Indian poet and scholar Muhammad Iqbal (d. 1938), who argued passionately in his *Reconstruction of Religious Thought in Islam*, "The only alternative open to us, then, is to tear off from Islam the hard crust which has immobilized an essentially dynamic outlook on life, and to rediscover the original verities of freedom, equality, and solidarity with a view to rebuild our moral, social and political ideas out of their original simplicity and universality" (156).

Asghar notes with irony that it seems to be the *Shari'ah* provisions on marriage and divorce, on maintenance and inheritance, that preoccupy the conservative clerics today, while the often progressive and even radical *Shari'ah* instructions on matters of economic justice, on fair trade and property law, are left to be decided by the legal codes inherited from Western colonialism.

It is time we take a turn toward the positive. What are the resources—besides the general good will of the *Qur'an*—that can be used in Islam by men and women who advocate gender justice? Preeminent is the simple fact that, unlike the sacred texts of Hinduism and Christianity, the founding texts of Islam are not written by nor do they recommend the lifestyle of celibate clerics and gurus. The *Qur'an* is replete with praises of the blessings of marriage, the accepted and expected way of adult life. "And among His signs is that he created for you [men and women] spouses from your own selves in order that you may have comfort in them and create between you love and mercy" (Q. 30).

Contrary to the fear and suspicion of sexuality in many other religious traditions, Islam insists upon the joint responsibility of husbands and wives for their mutual sexual pleasuring. The sexes are naturally drawn to one another, and what is natural cannot be against the sacred. Thus, even in the month of Ramadan, the fasting month, the *Qur'an* admonishes, "Going into your wives on the night of fasting is lawful for you. They are a garment for you and you are a garment for them" (Q. 2:185).

Concerning sexuality and family life, there is nothing of the world-denying asceticism of either Hinduism or early Christianity in Islam. Not the lonely forest dweller, not the celibate priest or monk or nun, but a happily married man and woman is the ideal in Islam—a life of good food, good sex, abundant harvests, loyal friends, and many children and grandchildren. Yes, early Islam is clearly a patriarchy. But it is a patriarchy much like Judaism, a patriarchy that enjoys the pleasures of this life without guilt. After all, the reward in the afterlife promised by Islam is a garden paradise. We find injustice toward women in Islam but never the ontological fear that sees in the bodies of women the danger of stain and pollution. Instead: "Humankind, fear your Lord who created you all from a single soul and from it He created its mate, and from them both He scattered about many men and women" (Q. 4). Islam affirms women as both gender companions and as lifelong partners who are to be honored and embraced with gratitude.

A second important positive resource in Islam for gender justice is the fact that, like Christianity, it is a worldwide religion. The clear majority of Muslims today are not even of Arab origin. There are more Muslims in Indonesia, for example, than in the entire Middle East. The most populous Muslim countries are all in Asia; they include Indonesia, India, Pakistan, Bangladesh, and China. There is a plurality of cultures and of practices concerning the social position of women. Take the matter of dress with which we began this chapter. Muslim women in Indonesia feel free to wear full-body covering or Western jeans and t-shirts. Some refuse to swim in mixed company, while others swim in common pools in two-piece bathing suits. There is simply no *ijma* (consensus) about these matters in this largest of Muslim countries. Or take the case of Kelantan, the most intensely Islamic of the states of the federation of Malaysia. There the women conduct the business activity, often in food markets, while men hold a conspicuously secondary economic position.

There is no clear or simple geography of gender in Islam, any more than there is any coherence concerning the identity and social role of women among Coptic Christians in Egypt, Catholic Christians in the Congo, or Protestant Christians in Boston. Islam benefits from a variety of ways of being Islamic. The question of gender justice in Islam presented in the Western media is often imaged, and therefore imagined, in terms of the practices of the most conservative nations in the Middle East. There is a reason for that, of course. It has to do with domestic and international politics—the politics of seeing and the politics of knowing. But the truth is that Islam, as an international collage of believers, is, like Christianity, not simply a collage but a broken and scattered mixture—a marvelous weave of contradictions.

Both Asghar and Farid find comfort and promise in Islam's obvious pluralism, which is rooted in the earliest practices of their faith. From the beginning, and against local custom, women in Islam enjoyed equal rights of divorce. In fact the prophet permitted a woman called Jamila to divorce her husband, against his will and without his consent, simply because she did not approve of his looks! The *Qur'an* (9:71) emphasizes that both believing men and believing women are to enjoin the good and forbid evil. From this, Asghar points out that jurists like Abu Hanifa concluded that women could become *Qadi* (judges) since their moral responsibility was equal to that of men. There is no instruction in the *Qur'an* that women should veil their faces; most Muslim women neither veil their faces nor cover their heads. In terms of their rights in marriage, decisions concerning their dress, and their right to earn money or to take an active role in public life, Muslim women today enjoy not a new freedom but rights embedded in their most ancient religious traditions.

While not abandoning his criticism of the male voice and the implied male audience of the *Qur'an*, Farid Esack, like Asghar Ali Engineer, finds abundant positive resources in the *Qur'an* for those seeking justice for women. The key, he claims, is to understand that the *Qur'an* is a text concerned overwhelmingly with God. It is fundamentally a theological text, not a text about legislation. Out of more than 6,000 verses, only some 230 address questions of legislation. Concerning the Qur'anic view of God, Farid singles out three attributes as central: *Tawhid* (Divine Unity), *Subhaniyyat* (Transcendence), and *Rububiyyat* (the Divine Sustaining Presence). All these bear positively on the issue of gender and justice.

Tawhid refers not simply to the unity of God but to the unity of all creation under the divine Lordship. *Tawhid* requires a holistic and fully integrated approach both in human worship and in human behavior, "a struggle" Farid calls it "to repair the wholeness of creation." Issues of justice cannot be separated one from the other. Justice for women involves issues of poverty and economic justice, issues of public participation and political justice, as well as the embracing issue of the rights of other-than-human living things or environmental justice. (We will find that Native American religions are especially helpful in discovering our enduring kinship and interdependence with the "more-than-human" species that share our world.) The *Tawhid* of God, Farid suggests, directly challenges the misogynistic idolatry that would in practice replace God for women with man, whom women are therefore to obey unquestioningly.

Farid argues that *Subhaniyyat*, the Divine Transcendence, undercuts any attempt to elevate law to some timeless or eternal status. God is *Akbar*—the "eternally greater than," or, in the words of the *Qur'an*, "God is free from what they ascribe unto him." What we find here is a bracing humility that undercuts human pretensions to insight (in law, for example) that aspires to a place of veneration above and beyond the given conditions of a particular time and place. To put it simply, God is greater than law; thus, *Subhaniyyat* liberates law to creative reinterpretation. Indeed, all human understanding is rendered relative and unfinished before the transcendent. As such, theology too is unfinished, an ongoing task of discernment, a still-in-the-making response to, not a repository of, revelation.

The *Qur'an*, Farid argues, portrays the transcendent deity as one who is also intimately engaged in the affairs of this world. That is why prophets are sent not all at once but over time—as instruments of God's progressive revelation. Farid points to the principle of *tadrij*, which implies that injunctions have been revealed gradually, reflecting the creative interaction between God's will and the ever-shifting realities of human social life. What is true for the *Qur'an* is even truer for all merely human interpretive acts. Every interpretation of a text is in a sense new, reflecting the times, circumstances, and personality of the interpreter. Interpretation is by its very nature a risk, at best a partial attempt at obedient discernment, always leaving itself open to later interpreters who bring their own, also partial viewpoints, because as humans that is all we can do. Letting God be God means we humans must be content to be human. For Islam, Farid concludes, it is forbidden (a violation of divine *Subhaniyyat*) to hold one generation as the intellectual hostage of another.

Finally, there is *Rububiyyat*. God is *rabb al-nas,* "that being who brings into life and nurtures until perfection." While law is implied in this, people as repositories of God's creative spirit both precede the law and are the horizon toward which law struggles *(jihad).* This struggle is guided by two inviolable principles: *Karamah* (the dignity intrinsic to each person), which requires *'ahalah* (justice). This notion of the creative Spirit of God—"always bringing into life and nurturing it towards perfection"—combined with *Karamah,* the dignity of all persons, stands as a powerful guard against the male paternalism that would treat women as perpetual minors, always remaining in need of male protection and supervision because "they" (women as object not as subject) are unable to take care of themselves. Paternalism is misogyny with a smiling face. Behind the smiles is men's fear of the full adulthood and self-direction of women—something that violates both *rabb* (the Divine Spirit in women) and *Karamah* (the dignity women enjoy equally with men).

Precisely this is why men must listen *to* women rather than talk among themselves *about* women. Even when talking about "what men owe women," we men are on dangerous ground. It is more honest and accurate to speak about what we owe ourselves as men. We owe it to our own dignity to unveil and denounce sexism. We owe it to the *rabb,* to the Divine Spirit at work in us, to grow out of that childishness that finds the empowerment of women a threat to ourselves. It is not women but we men who need to "grow up."

Sexism is a male problem that becomes a problem for women because of the power we men have traditionally exercised in society.

What we men owe to women, therefore, is a struggle for our own liberation, a struggle *(jihad)* that we can carry on only in active collaboration with women who speak out and struggle to gain control to direct their own lives; to put it more Islamically, to struggle to find their own path of submission and obedience. One thing seems clear: For women there is no freedom, no self-directing of their lives, no submission that is their own submission, if they do not have control of their sexuality and reproduction. That is why, years ago, the *ulama* of Indonesia declared that family planning is legitimately "Islamic." Unfortunately, in this respect Indonesia has remained years ahead of many other Islamic societies.

Ali Asghar Engineer and Farid Esack agree that what men owe women is really no more and no less than what we owe ourselves: honesty and the struggle for a justice that liberates both genders from the degradations of sexism. *Karamah,* the dignity of all persons, obligates us to this shared journey. It is an act of submission to God, who is just and compassionate.

4. Judaism

JUDAISM, MORE PRECISELY JUDAISM AS IT IS PRACTICED in Israel today, has much in common with Islam. This is especially true when considering the lives of women and the obligations to live one's life under religious law. For both traditions, law and life under the law is not a matter of choice but of identity. Ze'ev Falk, an Orthodox rabbi, lived and taught and fought for women's rights in Israel. But he fought as a rabbi who argued his case based not on "human rights"—a discourse he considered both Western and secular—but on the basis of Torah, an ancient tradition that was his own.

Ze'ev Falk was rector of the Seminary of Jewish Studies in Jerusalem and will be our guide in this chapter. He may seem a strange, even limited guide to many readers. Such is the distance between the Orthodox discourse on gender in Israel and the same issue as it is discussed among Jews here in North America. Yet Laurie Zoloth-Dorfman, chair of social ethics and Jewish studies at San Francisco State University, who knew and studied with Ze'ev, wrote this upon his sudden and unexpected death: "It is very hard to imagine Judaism without him! We will miss him very, very much, as a leader, teacher, rabbi, legal scholar, and friend. Please, in your book, be sure to tell those who may not know how rare a man this one was, how daring, how much a *mensch,* and an elegant and kind one."

Her words invite us into the argument Ze'ev conducts with his fellow rabbis in Israel. Her own deep roots, she knows, are planted in the same soil and close by to Ze'ev. To be Jewish, however informed by the modern and postmodern discourse on gender, is to live the legacy of Torah. Ze'ev does not want to surrender to that legacy; he wants to argue with it. There is something very wrong, for example, about the situation where a woman in Israel today, whose husband refuses to grant her a divorce, finds her life in ruins

43

because of the effectiveness of her spouse's revenge and the complicity in that revenge of the rabbinic courts. Ze'ev also knows—and proclaims and writes—that rabbis in his nation who refuse to invite women into the study and exposition of Torah are not just foolish anachronisms, but by their actions betray the clear intent of the Torah they claim to venerate. Still, Ze'ev wants to argue with these rabbis, not ignore them. He wants to argue that both Torah and *halakhah* (rabbinical law) can be used, should be used, indeed, must be used positively in the pursuit of gender justice.

Let us begin with the striking claim that Ze'ev makes concerning the fundamental nature of Torah. It tells the story, Ze'ev says, of an unfinished and ongoing discussion between God and his people. It is not the story of some final and forever established law and of unquestioning submission to it. Rather, the Bible tells of an ancient people bold enough to bring their complaints to God, asking on the grounds of justice that he change his mind—change the law, change his previous practice. And Torah discloses that God responds—positively. Sometimes the people who do the complaining are women. Take the case of the daughters of Zelophehad (Num 27:1–7). Their father died, leaving no sons. The law as established by God said only sons could inherit. The daughters felt deprived of justice and brought their complaint to Moses. Moses took their case "to the Lord." And God replied that the daughters' complaint was justified. So the laws of inheritance were changed. Torah displays a God who is in search of justice, a God who responds to changing social and historical circumstances.

Even more daring, Torah tells us that it is not just the people who should "repent of their ways," but God can and does repent and change his ways. Ze'ev points to Exod 32:11-14, where Moses complains to God that he is allowing his people to perish in the wilderness. Moses reminds God of the promises he made to Abraham and to Isaac about the land that their children would inherit, those children who are now dying in the desert. Torah records that God took the complaint seriously: "And God repented of the evil which he had thought to do to his people." God listens and sometimes God changes his ways. God is not finished with himself.

That theology (that idea of God) strikes many modern believers as close to heretical. It is not the God they were taught to worship.

Quite true. As Ze'ev points out, the God of Torah is not "the God of the Philosophers," for whom God could only be God if possessing (and thereby possessed by) attributes of timeless truth and insight. Instead, Torah displays a God who walks with his people, a God "contaminated" by time, a Lord and ruler who subjects himself to history, to a future that is not known in advance. Yes, God has a plan, but it is a plan-in-the-making. The implication for every reading of Torah is human risk and responsibility to find what justice here and now requires—not the safe elegance of established certainty. As the prophet Micah put it (6:7-8): "Will the Lord be pleased with thousands of rams [for sacrifice], or with ten thousands of rivers of oil [for anointing]? Shall I give my first born for my transgressions . . . ? He hath shown you, O man, what is good and what is required of you, to do justice, to love mercy, and to walk humbly with your God." Justice, not the veneration of sacred practices, is what God requires—not excluding the sacred practice of reading sacred books. God relativizes the Bible, leaving it open to a future not yet known.

It is important to point out that it was the God of the philosophers, not the God of Torah, who eventually dominated the religious imagination of the West (another consequence of the extraordinary birth of Christianity). The God of the philosophers is outside of time, a God who knows and wills everything before it happens, a God who stands forever in the same place— immutable and all-knowing. This God leads some people today to announce a misplaced sense of certainty, claiming that in Revelations we find a divine prognostication of the present nuclear age, its environmental crisis, and the coming end of the world. Torah, Ze'ev reminds us, demands moral adulthood. And that means leaving behind the fictitious safety of divine foreknowledge in order to continue our dialogue with a Lord whose rule requires and awaits our human response and responsibility.

The God we walk with also walks with us.

The implications that Torah's view of the divine-human relationship brings to issues of gender justice are clear. And Ze'ev Falk says it boldly: "New Torah has to be written." He quotes from a book by Martin Buber on the medieval Jewish mystics, the *chassidim*. It is reported that a certain Simchah Bunew once said: "Moses in his benevolence had intended to reveal more than that

to the people, but was not allowed to do so. God wanted the people themselves, not Moses alone, to interpret Torah beyond its revealed text, so as to find Him in the act of creative interpretation" (Martin Buber, *Or Hag: Sippurey Chassidim* [Jerusalem: Schocken, 1957], 420). Having opened the tradition at its very core, how does Ze'ev carry on his dialogue with other rabbis in Israel today who, like Ze'ev, seek to remain obedient to the way of Torah?

Ze'ev opens that discussion by pointing out how profoundly everyday life has changed from the social conditions that existed when Torah and *halakhah* were being written. This is especially true for women. Traditionally and up until quite recently, Jewish women lived their lives enmeshed in the extended family. And the extended family did not have a fixed border but was embedded within the larger Jewish community. Everyday life was lived within a very tight weave. To uphold social discipline, besides the law, there were gossip and the ubiquitous surveillance of life lived in a narrowly circumscribed social setting. Within that tightly woven matrix, women enjoyed a degree of protection. They were never far removed from sisters or brothers or an appeal to the wider community. Men practiced patriarchy, but it was patriarchy under collective discipline.

Today the communal structure has disappeared in the daily life of the modern city. Of course it is possible to set up enclaves that seek to replicate the traditional ways. Many of the Orthodox—both in Israel and in our own country—attempt to build and preserve such intentional communities. However, most Jews, including most Jewish women, prefer to live in the anonymity and the autonomy of the secular city. And living under those more free but also more exposed circumstances, women need new Torah, a new interpretation. As modern women, they remain inheritors of the legacy, and their lives present new issues of justice to that legacy. What must be done, Ze'ev argues, is honestly to embrace the modern way of life and to engage in dialogue with Jewish women about what is required for justice and mercy in this new way of walking with God. For a genuinely two-way discussion, the tradition of confining the study and interpretation of Torah to men must be abandoned, obediently and joyfully abandoned. Women must be able to tell us men what we owe them under these new circumstances. And Torah must respond to their voices or cease to be the voice of Jewishness.

The active presence of women in the religious life of the community outside of the home has many biblical precedents. Ze'ev points to the Passover sacrifice that included both wives and daughters (Exod 12:3-20). Wives also participated in the annual pilgrimage to the central sanctuary (Deut 14:26; 15:20; 16:11; 1 Sam 1:9). In biblical times women could form their own spiritual practices. Wives, for example, could leave their husbands behind and take the Sabbath or New Moon meal at the table of the prophet (2 Kings 4:22-27). Under Joshua's leadership, women participated in the public celebration of the covenant (Josh 8:35), and at the time of Ezra women actively participated in the public reading of the Torah (Neh 8:2).

Concerning women's exclusion from the study of Torah, Ze'ev says that its recent roots can be traced to 64 C.E., when elementary schools for boys only were established in Judea and Galilee by the high priest Joshua ben Gamla. This gender-exclusive primary education led, in turn, to the establishment of all-male Talmud academies. Yet this practice of discrimination, Ze'ev argues, took place without strict legal justification. The issue of including or excluding women from the study of Torah was debated both in the Bible and in rabbinic tradition in relationship to the story recounted in Num 5:11-31 concerning "the ordeal of jealousy." If a husband suspected his wife of infidelity but had no proof, he could satisfy his jealousy by taking his wife before the priest who would prepare a "bitter drink" to test her. If as a result "her belly swelled" and "her thigh rotted," it was proof of her guilt. On the other hand, if the bitter drink passed through her without effect, it proved her innocence. But—and this is what became crucial to the debate concerning women's education—the teaching also included the warning that sometimes the test failed to detect the truth, and guilty women escaped. Ben Azzai and R. Eliezer ben Hyrcanos entered into debate about this warning in the second century. Ben Azzai argued that general knowledge of the teaching was obligatory; that is, women should be taught Torah. But R. Eliezer countered by saying that such knowledge would tempt women into immorality.

In no other case is it recorded that Eliezer's interpretation was favored. But in this case, it was accepted and eventually extended to prevent all study of Torah by women.

According to Ze'ev, from this highly dubious precedent women were not only excluded from study in general but also excluded from wearing phylacteries, from counting in the quorum needed for public prayer, and from playing an active role in the community. Women were disqualified as witnesses, as judges, and as community leaders. This sad tale of discrimination arose (as the biblical story just cited indicates) out of male suspicion and fear of female sexuality; it continued and expanded because of that fear. The Bible has no record of a "bitter drink" prepared by priests for men whose wives suspected them of infidelity!

Jewish women, Ze'ev argues, did not accept this gender bias and injustice passively. They resisted; they infiltrated territory reserved by *halakhah* for men. In the early Middle Ages, women joined men in drinking wine on Passover night and in lighting Hannukah candles. According to some authorities, women even led worship services, reading the megillah. Women subverted and invaded other formerly exclusionary practices such as the reading of Shema and prayers, participating in the Seder, counting the *Omer,* hearing the blowing of the shofar, sitting in the sukkah, and taking the *lulav* (palm branch). There is a long history of Jewish women's self-emancipation. His fellow Orthodox rabbis, Ze'ev says, need to hearken to this "subversive history" and set aside their attempts to maintain a gender monopoly over contemporary religious communal practices.

Actually, Ze'ev puts this a bit more strongly. Concerning the contemporary conduct of rabbinical courts in Israel, he quotes the prophet Amos: "I take no delight in your solemn assemblies. . . . Take away from me the noise of your songs, to the melody of your harps I will not listen. But let justice roll down like water and righteousness like an everlasting stream" (Amos 5:21-24). And he adds from Jeremiah: "The priests did not say, 'Where is the LORD?' Those who handle the law did not know me" (2:8). Strong words for what repentance and justice require concerning gender justice today.

Ze'ev cites a biblical passage that concerns the treatment of women taken captive in war. He uses it to illustrate the way Torah tries to protect the rights of women. Acknowledging the distance in time, I nevertheless want to quote this text in order to challenge Ze'ev's use of it as a positive precedent. The passage is found in Deut 21:10-14:

> When you go forth to war against your enemies . . . and see among the captives a beautiful woman . . . then you shall bring her home . . . and she shall . . . bewail her father and her mother a full month; after that you may go in to her, and be her husband, and she shall be your wife. Then, if you have no delight in her, you shall let her go where she will; but you shall not sell her for money, you shall not treat her as a slave, since you have humiliated her.

Knowing what was done to captive women in Bosnia and elsewhere in recent times, such an admonition does in fact seem a still-needed extension of protection to women caught on the losing side in war. But hidden within this seemingly benign biblical precedent is a problem we need to address: the pervasiveness of the male voice. God is presented (as usual!) talking to men about women and about how men (as positive actors) are to treat women (as passive recipients of the injunctions delivered to men). That God in the Bible speaks in a male voice to an audience clearly intended as male presents a fundamental issue to the reading of those texts for those who would be faithful to gender justice. Farid Esack addressed the issue concerning the *Qur'an,* and we need to follow his example and raise the same question with Torah. God is presented in these texts as usually talking to men and almost never talking to women, who remain the talked-about.

It is not enough to say, as Ze'ev says, that everyone knows that women are included in the benevolent regard of God. It is not enough to say that everyone knows that God wishes the best for women as well as for men. The male-to-male voice written into the text itself results in a fundamental and persisting bias. This is especially true when you consider the ritual use of the text and how its repeated reading has continued down the generations to voice that gender-biased voice in public worship. This biased voice, inscribed within our sacred texts, obliges us in the name of justice to open the space of religious ritual to the voice that up until now has been so systematically excluded. A quote from R. Levi Yitschaq of

Berditchev (1740–1809), cited by Ze'ev, can help us open this space. It reads: "We comprehend only the meaning of the black letters, but not the white gaps between the letters. There will come a time when God will reveal even the white hiddenness of Torah."

That time is now. Those empty spaces must be filled by the voices and writings of women, women fully trained in the tradition—trained in Torah, in Talmud, in rabbinic studies—but most of all trained by their own experience as women. This is already happening here in the United States. In the non-Orthodox denominations—Conservative, Reform, and Reconstructionist—the training of Jewish women in religious scholarship and their preparation as congregational rabbis have taken firm hold. Even the Orthodox communities show movement. In Israel, for example, Ze'ev points out that Orthodox women trained in Torah and *halakhah*, as examined and certified by the Chief Rabbinate of Israel, have been appointed "rabbinic pleaders" to argue before (the still all-male) rabbinic courts. Moreover, as Orthodox feminist Blu Greenberg has noted: "The confluence of women's learning in Orthodoxy with the model of female rabbis in the other movements will lead to women becoming Orthodox rabbis, although probably not pulpit rabbis." Already in Israel, Orthodox women are chanting the blessing over wine and the havdalah at home and saying the mourner's prayer during the year-long mourning period. As Greenberg concludes, "The taboos against seeing and hearing women perform communal acts of holiness are steadily being lifted." Still, progress is far from automatic and requires constant struggle, as was made clear by the physical assault by Orthodox rabbis on women trying to pray with men at the Western Wall in Jerusalem.

In non-Orthodox synagogues, new liturgies for the birth of a daughter and to celebrate other life events of women are becoming common. Discussion about the sexist language in prayer, Scripture, and tradition is leading to liturgical reform and to the use of gender-inclusive language in worship. However, one area needs more recognition than it has received so far. It concerns Jewish women who decide to live a single life. Rabbinic law, Ze'ev admits, has until now addressed women's lives as if their only legitimate goals were marriage and motherhood. But today, education, the opening up of new careers, the availability of contraception, later marriages, a rising divorce rate, and Jewish women affirming their alternative sexual orientation raise issues of community recognition and liturgical innovation for celebrating life events that differ from the past. It is not enough to leave the more contentious of these issues to civil law to settle. Jewish women who choose to live their lives in continuity with both Torah and tradition require innovative religious practices, new laws, and new traditions created by and celebrated in the community. This new creativity continues the way of walking with God that was recorded first in ancient texts and has continued ever since.

In this task of pursuing gender justice, Judaism, like Islam, is blessed with a heritage that positively affirms sexuality and sexual pleasuring. The Jewish faith affirms that women and men are born of sex and are naturally oriented toward sex, that sexuality is not temptation requiring suspicion but a natural drive deserving to be satisfied. Ze'ev quotes Torah: "When a man has taken a new wife, he shall not go out to war, neither shall he be charged with any business; but he shall be free at home one year, and shall bring cheer to his wife which he has taken" (Deut 24:5). It should be noted that the emphasis here is not on procreation but on mutual sexual pleasuring and the bonds of friendship nurtured thereby. Given that emphasis, it does not appear that the affirmation of the text should be limited to the language of "man" and "wife," but should be interpreted to include all faithful relationships.

Jewish women living in modern society are confronted with all the decisions concerning sexual practices that confront other women. These include decisions about premarital and postmarital sex as well as issues of abortion and of artificial insemination both for infertile couples and for single or partnered women who want to become mothers. Same-sex partnering and the celebration of these unions in public worship are probably the most controversial of these issues at present. Jewish women are making decisions about these issues, so new interpretations of Torah and *halakhah* are needed.

When faced with controversial issues, by what principles should the community be guided as it pursues both sexual justice and gender justice? We can turn to Torah. In Deut 1:16-17, we find this admonition from God: "Hear *the causes* between your people, and judge justly between every person, including the stranger amongst you. Do not judge by appearance, but hear equally the weak and the strong, for it is God who is the judge. And if a case be too difficult, then bring that case to me and I will hear it and decide it" (emphasis added).

The principles of justice and of just decisions in new and difficult cases are clear. First, examine without bias what issues are at stake. In that task, do not discriminate between that which is familiar and that which is strange. This requires that you ignore given social distinctions and appearances because they will always reflect how power is exercised in society, and just judgments can only arise when liberated from the domination of the strong. Be bold, especially in deciding for the stranger or for those whose appearance differs from the accepted norms, because justice is from God, not from what is human. Where you find no certainty as to what justice requires, do not rely upon the past or on what has previously been decided. Instead, bring the case to a new hearing and learn what God in this new time requires you to do so that justice will be served.

It is hard to conceive of a more solid foundation to pursue issues of gender justice. The stranger made strange in the tradition, the weak abused by the powerful in the tradition, the body made polluted in the tradition, the voice that in order to be heard had to appeal to God above and beyond previous practices in the tradition—these have always been women. So let us males put the bitter drink of the "ordeal of jealousy" behind us. In all justice, we should not fear the power of women or punish them any longer for their God-given desire for freedom and self-determination. We need the voice of women in order to come into a more honest relationship with ourselves as men. It is not women who compromise or contaminate us, but our own minds. We should hearken, therefore, to the words of the psalmist (from the King James translation):

> The fear of the LORD is clean[sing],
>> enduring for ever:
> The judgments of the LORD are true
>> and righteous altogether.
> More to be desired are they than
>> gold,

Yea, than much fine gold:
Sweeter also than honey and the
honeycomb.

(Ps 19:9-10)

Gold—the power to dominate—does not and cannot feed us, but honey can and does. And its sweetness can wash our hearts clean.

We may conclude where we began—with Ze'ev Falk arguing the case for gender justice with his fellow rabbis in Jerusalem. Concerning the issue of divorce, Ze'ev argues that a special *taqqunah* should be made by the Chief Rabbinate annulling the marriage where a wife is faced with a husband who refuses to authorize the delivery of a letter of divorce. Unless and until that *taqqunah* is made, jurisdiction over the termination of marriages should be vested in the supreme court of the state. There should be no rules concerning the modesty of women's dress that do not apply fully and equally to men. Thus, if the hair and face of Jewish women are to be covered, the same must apply to the hair and face (including the beard) of Jewish men.

The separation of the genders in synagogue worship should either be ended or a parallel service without separation should be offered everywhere as an alternative. Finally, both sexes must join the struggle in Israel for equal access to public office by women, to an equal share of political power for women, and to an equal partnership of women in the rabbinate, in rabbinical courts, and in the whole domain of public worship and religious administration.

For all of us who struggle for gender justice, but especially for those who struggle in Israel, the voice of Ze'ev Falk will be sorely missed.

5. Buddhism

WHEN INTERROGATING RELIGIONS ON A SPECIFIC ISSUE, as we are doing in this book, it is wise to begin with a self-consciously chosen point of entrance. It reminds both the reader and the writer that the interest is not general (say, an introduction to the religion) but specific and focused. We did that with Judaism by likening the discussion of gender and justice in that tradition to the way contemporary Islam talks about religious law and the lives of women. In discussing Islam, we illustrated how the Western reader is likely to bring a biased point of view and argued that case with an analysis of contemporary female dress. We began our discussion of Christianity with a description of that religion's astonishing start— its reincarnation from its Jewish beginnings into a Greco-Roman religion, and what that meant regarding the Christian view of the human body.

In approaching Buddhism—a religion that spread eastward from India, first across Indochina and then throughout all of East Asia—we will follow a similar strategy. We will turn to modern Thailand and choose as our point of entrance the issue of prostitution among young, poor, rural girls in the burgeoning sex trade of Bangkok. We will look at the tragedy of AIDS in that country, where local health experts tell us that 50 percent of the prostitutes in the capital city are HIV positive. In Thailand's second largest city, Chiang Mai, half the hospital beds are filled with those dying of AIDS, mostly women in their twenties or early thirties. While the primary culprits in this cruel drama are rural poverty, corrupt local politicians, and the military who "purchase" or "contract" the young girls from their families, Theravada Buddhism has been remarkably complacent about the practice of prostitution for generations. In more recent times, Buddhism has remained mostly silent about the tragic application of the traditional virtue of "filial piety" and its role in recruiting these young girls.

Our guide will be Tavivat Puntarigvivat, a scholar of comparative religion at Mahidol University in Bangkok. We will begin with this puzzle: How could a religious tradition like Buddhism, which arose as a protest against the injustices of the caste system in Hinduism and innovated a program for the ordination of women—who were viewed as endowed with religious promise as fully as men—become so mired in gender injustice? How could such a promising beginning result in the current silence and complacency of Buddhist monks before the deaths of so many young women in Thailand?

As with other religions, the discrepancy is both astonishing—given the attitudes and actions of the founder—and, retrospectively, quite easy to predict. In the time of Siddhartha Gautama the Buddha, some 2,500 years ago, it was considered a misfortune when a daughter was born instead of a son. The story is told that King Kosala was in the midst of a conversation with the Buddha when news came that his wife, Mallika, had given birth to a daughter, and the king grew visibly upset. But the Buddha responded:

> Do not be perturbed, O King,
> A female child may prove
> Even a better offspring than a male,
> for she may grow up wise and virtuous.
> (*Kindred Sayings*, I:iii)

The Buddha taught his disciples that "to respect one's mother and one's wife is to be blessed." This respect should be something general, not confined to family members. Thus, Buddhist texts tell us to treat every woman as "your own mother or sister," and refer to women in general as "a society of mothers" *(matugama)*. Most importantly, the Buddha taught that women were equal to men in their capacity to attain Nirvana; both were equally endowed religiously with the capacity for enlightenment. In speaking of enlightenment, Buddha likens the way to a chariot and says:

> And be it woman, be it man for whom
> Such chariot does wait, by that same car
> Into *Nibbana*'s presence shall they come.
> (*Kindred Sayings*, I:45)

Even more crucial for the future of Buddhist women, Tavivat claims, is the story of Maha Pajapati Gotami, Siddhartha's aunt.

When his mother died seven days after his birth, Gotami took over the raising of the child who would one day become Buddha. Many years later, upon the death of her husband King Suddhodana, Siddhartha's father, Gotami renounced the world; after a long and difficult journey on foot, she found the Buddha and asked him for ordination. At first, Buddha refused. But his faithful disciple Ananda—who after Buddha's death would be denounced by his fellow monks for this action—intervened on Gotami's behalf. After seeing her persist three times without success, Ananda asked the Buddha, "Lord, are women capable, after going forth from the home unto the homeless life under the Norm-Discipline set forth by the Tathagata—are they capable of realizing the Fruit of Stream-winning, of Once-returning, of Never-returning, of Arahantship?" Buddha replied: "Women are capable . . . of doing so, Ananda." Whereupon Ananda replied:

> Then, Lord, if women are capable . . . of so doing, inasmuch as Maha-Pajapati, the Gotamind, was of great service to the Exalted One—for she was aunt, nourisher, and milk-giver, on the death of his mother she suckled the Exalted One—well were it, Lord, if women were permitted to go forth from home unto the homeless life under the Norm-Discipline set forth by the Tathagata.

The Buddha then relented and granted Gotami full ordination.

Whether fiction or a remembered reality, the truth of the story is in its being part of the sacred record that establishes Buddhism. It records the founding, alongside the male Bhikkhu Sangha, of the Bhikkhuni Sangha or order of Buddhist nuns—the first institution-alization of an independent religious life for women in the history of world religions. The innovation persisted despite strong objections by the monks after Buddha's death. Many Buddhist women followed the path opened for them by their founder and are remembered as having joined the Bhikkhuni institution by the thousands, leaving for later generations stories of female lives dedicated to religion and led by women. Such memories continue to inspire Buddhist women today, as witnessed by the flourishing of Buddhist nuns in Taiwan, where the women who become nuns—not to leave but to stay and serve the needy in this world—are often of high educational and secular career attainments. From its

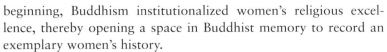

beginning, Buddhism institutionalized women's religious excellence, thereby opening a space in Buddhist memory to record an exemplary women's history.

However, this auspicious beginning also includes a downside. It concerns the Eight Important Rules *(gurudharma)*, which are remembered as having been imposed by the Buddha himself upon women who would become nuns. Given the historic hostility of the majority of monks to the Bhikkhuni, these rules may well be a later invention. Again, the truth of the memory is found in its being remembered, therefore taking on social power. In effect, the Eight Important Rules attributed to the Buddha and imposed upon those who become nuns rescind much of women's claim to equal religious status. The rules oblige subservience by nuns to male monks, instructing them never to find fault but always to show respect and never to complain, even among themselves, about their treatment by the monks. Another of the rules responds to the ancient male suspicion of female sexuality and counsels pervasive male surveillance and control. Finally, it is reported that Buddha told Ananda that the establishment of the institution of Buddhist nuns would be costly to their religion, cutting its lifespan in half (from one thousand to five hundred years)—a prediction disproved by time.

Buddhist scriptures were finally written down and recorded nearly four hundred years after the death of the Buddha. Scholars today believe that the scriptures underwent significant redaction, responding to the continuing deep suspicion, competition, and hostility of monks toward nuns. After all, they were men who had chosen to live celibate lives, who viewed marriage as distinctly second class. They had fled the world to escape desire; now living a shared lifestyle with them were nuns.

Political events in India and Sri Lanka in the eleventh century led to the extinction of the tradition of the Bhikkhuni in Thailand, although the tradition was to pass successfully into China, Korea, Japan, and modern Taiwan. The result is that today Buddhist women in Thailand are deprived of the option to live their lives within religious community, under the supervision of other women, engaged in service to others and gaining education. This historic fact interacts negatively with the tradition of filial piety that bears upon the lives of Thai young women, although once married they enjoy considerable leverage within their culture's family system.

The system is matrilineal and privileges links between mothers and daughters rather than between fathers and sons. A scholar of Thai family structure, Chatsumarn Kabilsingh, comments:

> Under the system of corvee labor in the Ayudhya period, [Thai] men would be away from their homes at least every other month, sometimes for as long as three months. During their absence, women took care of the families. Because of this, it was customary for newly married couples to live with the wife's family. This led to a matrilineal social system and also to relative financial independence for women.

This legacy is still strong today. Thai farm women often provide the major portion of family income through their market activity, control the family purse strings, and are the voice of the family in village government. However, in an increasingly tragic irony, because of the earlier male work rules that enforced long absences from their wives, Thai men enjoy cultural immunity for sexual practices with prostitutes—an immunity they and their wives do not enjoy when it comes to AIDS.

The situation now facing rural Thai women presents us with a structurally complex picture and problem. Most of them are poor and will remain poor for the rest of their lives. They enjoy certain cultural privileges within the family but have been denied by history any significant or publicly visible participation in the religious life of the community. It is a contradictory situation, Tavivat contends, that demands structural analysis. That is why he is highly critical of the seemingly progressive thought of recent religious reformers in Thailand like Buddhadassa, who tried to work out a theory of "Dharmic Socialism." Buddhadassa's works, Tavivat complains, are filled with well-meaning admonitions and well-presented theological arguments concerning the rights of the poor, but they lack any analysis of how power works in society. The result is that they remain pious sentiments offering no hope for true reform.

Perhaps that is not accidental. Max Weber, the brilliant sociologist of religion, distinguishes between two strikingly different systems of religious thought. What separates them, Weber argues, is the social-class origin of those who produce the ideas. In the prophetic religions, it was persons of relatively unprivileged classes that produced theories of salvation based upon "a theodicy of recompense"—anticipating, for example, a coming Messianic age when the fortunes of this world would be reversed "and the last would become first."

Over against this kind of "theology from below," we find religious ideas originating from privileged classes that typically posit a very different notion of liberation, displaying what Weber calls "a theodicy of deservedness." These systems tend toward practices of elitist self-cultivation; they look to an eventual release from all concerns for life in this world. While containing an ethic of personal benevolence and rectitude, in pursuit of personal perfection such elitist conceptions of salvation tend to ignore and bypass structural analysis of how power works in society. Tavivat is convinced that Buddhism must add to its traditional person-centered ethic a new "subversive" social ethic that analyzes structural violence—the violence done by people who enjoy a high degree of social repute but who also control to their own benefit the institutions—including the religious institutions—that shape everyday life.

Contemporary issues of gender justice in Thailand, Tavivat claims, are inextricably woven into the fabric of the established political economy, a neocolonial economy of the Western global hegemony. Economic development strategies support industrial and agricultural activity for export at the expense of the urban and rural poor. In countries like Thailand—somewhere between "developing" and "industrialized"—national economies are responsive to the economic interests of the older industrial or now postindustrial societies of the West. The reason? Investment capital from the West decides which economic activity in the "two-thirds world" will be funded and flourish and which will be left to flounder.

Both the urban and the rural economies of these in-between countries are steered by the logic of profits, by foreign investors remorselessly searching to maximize their short-term returns. In response, national manufacturing in those countries focuses not on local needs for appropriate technology (pollution-controlled motorbikes, for example), but on commodities produced for foreign consumers (consumers who have money to buy computers or high-fashion sports sneakers). In rural areas, once agricultural production has been fully integrated into the global market, food follows profits. In northern Thailand, for example, small farmers find themselves displaced by an agribusiness that uses their land—once planted in rice for local subsistence markets—to cultivate fruits and vegetables intended for winter export to consumers in Japan and Europe. As a result, green beans and oranges will be cheaper to buy in December in Tokyo than produce from California, while the supply of rice in northern Thailand will be reduced—with the predictable consequence of becoming more expensive.

Reversing the logic of justice, global capitalism makes food cheaper for the well-to-do even as it makes food more expensive for the poor. Such structural injustices, Tavivat argues, require critical analysis and structural responses at the level of social policy—in short, a new Buddhist social ethics.

Such fundamental policy changes depend in turn upon the voice of the poor getting power at the national level: in other words, democracy. Real democracy has less to do with global free markets than with markets responsive and responsible to local people and their needs, people who are mostly poor, who are structurally ignored in the global search for profits. What democracy entails, then, is open and competitive local elections uncorrupted by "money politics," elections that pose real economic alternatives for public debate and decision. And what that requires is an end to the power of corrupt indigenous elites, an end to their cronyism and to their nepotism, an end to restrictive labor-organizing policies, and an end to the politics of managing local disappointment of the masses by turning it into anger at local religious minorities. Positively, it requires a judiciary responsive to the needs of all the people, not just the needs of the special people, as well as an active national economic planning board with monetary policies that protect against international currency speculators.

In rural areas, democratic reform would mean land reform and new rural development policies. It would mean a system of microcredit available in places like rural Thailand, where women have for generations developed entrepreneurial skills responsive to village markets. It would mean public investment in public health—infrastructure investments in clean public water, in improved sanitation, and in public health clinics where women can get free treatment for their children and effective family planning to help them keep themselves and their live children alive in the future.

But this kind of fundamental change, Tavivat knows, depends finally upon a truly fundamental recovery, a recovery of indigenous culture, a recovery of a public respect and admiration and emulation not programmed by global media and its advertising. Since the heart of culture lies in religion, the struggle for those of us who seek justice is, in the end, a battle over ultimate loyalties. That battle is not between the older religions but between all of them together and a new religion. The struggle against AIDS (a war now being lost), the struggle for the well-being of women (the majority of whom are poor), and the struggle for global gender justice (including justice to our mother Earth) will be fought—indeed are being fought—on the battlefield of religion.

The claim will strike some as foolish. However, Japanese Buddhist scholar David Loy clarifies the argument. In "The Religion of the Market" (*Visions of a New Earth*, ed. Harold Coward and Daniel C. Maguire [Albany: SUNY Press, 2000], 15–28), Loy points out that, if we define religion functionally as that which grounds our lives by teaching us what the world *is* and therefore what our role in that world *should be*, then it is obvious that traditional religions everywhere are being overwhelmed. Another and different explanation of what is really real, and what really counts, and what we need to do and to be if we really want to count, is taking the place of the traditional religions. Loy calls it "the religion of the market." As any religion must, this new religion presents to us a definitive worldview, one based on science and the laws of science, especially of the master science of economics. It also presents us with a new ethos, a center of value that assigns everything else its value, in relationship to which we learn our own value.

Economics functions today, Loy claims, as a new theology. It effectively steers the world and represents itself as understanding, mastering, and thus fully qualified to do that steering. The laws of economics are presented as objective, like the laws of physics. It is both futile and self-contradictory not to obey such laws. And everywhere this new worldview, which organizes our view of reality, is reflected back to us by its construction of the material culture that surrounds us. The reality and rightness of the global market becomes the same world in which we live— materially enmeshed in our everyday lives.

Tavivat saw that happening in rural Thailand, where he had lived first as a monk and later as a young scholar writing a book. Those who could hardly afford to feed their own families fed him daily—a custom of religious respect. But he began to witness a new and very different custom of respect, a consumerism that led some to sell a daughter into prostitution—not to buy food for the family or a new water buffalo, but to buy a prized motorbike. There, in that poor and rural village that graciously cared for him as a (male) monk and scholar, Tavivat had his eyes opened. The global market, responding to the need for access to agricultural products and raw materials in developing countries, built roads and strung electric lines that snaked their way into the remotest villages. But roads, Tavivat saw, travel two ways. It takes local produce out and brings outside produce in. Electricity puts a television into a village shop where in the evening all the village comes to watch. And what goes out (as produce) and what comes in (as culture) receives its value from the global market.

We can witness what Tavivat saw closer to home. In cities around the world, we see new places of worship—the biggest and busiest buildings in town. Not temples, not mosques, not cathedrals, not castles, not courts of law, not city halls—but shopping malls! Here is where people bring their hopes and their fears—even if those hopes and fears can do no more than look longingly from a distance, like a congregation watching the drama in the chancel up front or women listening to men reading and talking to other men about God's word.

Loy argues that this new religion of the market is the most aggressively successful missionary religion the world has ever seen, gaining more converts in one hundred years than Christianity or Islam or Buddhism could win in a thousand. It is no wonder. This new religion has an annual missionary budget (called global advertising) that dwarfs what any single nation spends on education in a year. Like all successful missionary religions, it creates an insatiable need for more ritual practices, for further reassurance. At every level of devotion and sacrifice, it leaves us still unsure, still anxious, still needing more.

Over one hundred years ago American sociologist Thorstein Veblen diagnosed a contagion he saw beginning to colonize human hearts and minds. He called it "conspicuous consumption." It was a new kind of consuming—a satisfaction sought not directly (as in buying an apple to eat it) but indirectly, a satisfaction sought from the public repute that ownership and the conspicuous display of that commodity confers. It led inevitably, Veblen reasoned, to an ethos of "obligatory ostentation"—each of us, running alongside everyone else, watching one another's "pile of stuff" out of the corner of our eye, deciphering thereby "how well we are doing." Every level of stuff (and it doesn't have to be a new car but only new sneakers or for some even new laces for old sneakers) becomes immediately unsatisfying. In that race for repute, we can never reach a place where we have enough, where we are enough, where we can belong to the self *we already are*—no longer driven and controlled by desire that always leaves us desiring again. The religion of the market is a marvelously closed and fully functional circle, a science of reality (a worldview) that supports a way of life (an ethos) that constantly feeds back and fuels the worldview—a certifiable miracle from the perspective of the sociology of religion.

The lives of poor women in Thailand and the critical and structural analysis required of those who would respond to that condition with gender justice can find in Buddhist doctrine a powerful and positive resource. Both Loy and Tavivat argue that, by using Buddhism as an instrument of diagnosis and prescription, one can gain the interpretive high ground in understanding the deep root of that perpetual dis-ease that the religion of the market sells around the world as salvation. False religious promises can best be unveiled by comparing them to religious doctrines that hold closer to the truth concerning the human condition, embodied in Buddhism in the Four Noble Truths.

Buddhism understands life as fundamentally impermanent and transient. We experience this inescapable reality as suffering (*Dukkha*) because of our clinging, our desiring, our trying to hold on. Nirvana (Tavivat's *Nibbana*) is its cure, and is spoken about in this way:

> Enraptured with lust *(raga)*, enraged with anger *(dosa)*, blinded by delusion *(moha)*, overwhelmed, with mind ensnared, man aims at his own ruin, at the ruin of others, at the ruin of both, and he experiences mental pain and grief. But if lust, anger,

and delusion are given up, man aims neither at his own ruin, nor at the ruin of others, nor at the ruin of both, and he experiences no mental pain and grief. Thus is Nirvana visible in this life, immediate, inviting, attractive, and comprehensible to the wise. (*Anguttara Nikaya* III.55)

At the heart of the religion of the market is acquisitive individualism, a self endlessly seeking its own interests and satisfactions. For Buddhism, that is the Great Illusion. The self as a permanent being, as a center that can collect things over time and hold on to those things, and find identity through what is being held onto—that is the great illusion that causes suffering. Instead, Buddhism teaches the doctrine of "no-self" *(anātmān)*. It is argued in this way:

> In the absolute sense, beings have only a very short moment to live, life lasting as long as a single moment of consciousness lasts. Just as a cart wheel, whether rolling or whether at a standstill, at all times only rests on a single point of its periphery: even so the life of a living being lasts only for the duration of a single moment of consciousness. As soon as the moment ceases, the being also ceases. For it is said: "The being of the past moment of consciousness has lived, but does not live now, nor will it live in the future. The being of the future moment has not yet lived, nor does it live now; but it will live in the future. The being of the present moment has not lived, it does live just now, but will not live in the future. (*The Path of Purification*, p. 256)

Buddhism pictures this truth to itself in what is called "the Wheel of Becoming"—the *samsara* or endless cycling that causes "greed, hatred, and delusion." These are literally pictured at the wheel's center in terms of animals: the cock, the snake, and (let us note) the pig. Craving, grasping—trying to buy, pile up, hold onto in order to be held up—all this is "delusion." To this ceaseless disease, Buddhism offers a counter-prescription: "This is the Noble Truth concerning the Cessation of Suffering; verily, it is passionlessness, cessation without remainder of this very craving; the laying aside of, the giving up, the being free from, the harboring no longer of, this craving" (*Vinaya Texts*, I:95).

It is hard to imagine a teaching more subversive of the very foundations of the religion of the market, with its assumptions about human motivations and the nature of human satisfaction—endlessly needing, wanting, grasping, holding.

In what sense is any of this of direct help to the poor women of Thailand? How does it offer resources for gender justice? Tavivat points out that the prostituting of young daughters has several causes. One of them is the spreading contagion of conspicuous consumption that has fully infected even the poorest families living in the most remote and destitute villages of the north. And it has infected not just the parents. The daughter, too, may suffer from the illusion that in offering herself in "filial piety" to the well-being of the family, she will be able to enjoy the fruits of her labor by giving monetary gifts to the family back home and by buying for herself the pretty dresses, the creamy skin, the shiny black hair she sees on television. The cultural silence concerning prostitution, along with the cultural silence about AIDS, invites such illusionary hopes among young women.

But the realities of rural poverty, the lack of opportunity for uneducated women, and the obvious market for the sex trade has led some Western interpreters, who think of themselves as progressive and level-headed, to view this life option as not so unrealistic. Prostitution seems not so different from the work wives traditionally do in support of the male ego; it pays better, without the added burden of housework and children. That opinion has faded as the full dimensions of the AIDS epidemic have become clear, and the coercive practices of corrupt police and government officials have been documented, but it raises the serious issue of realistic life options for poor women facing the realities of survival in the developing world.

One option is to become a factory worker. Young girls are viewed with special favor by the burgeoning electronics and microchip industries. Work that requires hours behind microscopes each day benefits from young eyes (though the eyes do not stay young for long). Also, young women, having been educated by a culture that values them less than males, have lower expectations for wages and working conditions. They dream of their futures in terms of love and marriage and children and see their present work as temporary and not worth a struggle or fight. Even if they should decide to fight, multinational corporations, confronting successful organizing activity, can easily move to the country next door. This has caused those seeking international gender justice to put new emphasis upon international bodies like the United Nations and the International Labor Organization, so that policies ensuring economic rights for women can be pursued across national borders.

Tavivat argues that there is another and, in the immediate future, more promising life option for poor rural girls in Thailand. And that involves the revival of the order of Buddhist nuns that has been absent from that country since the eleventh century but has survived and thrived elsewhere. If given this option, young girls could choose to enter the Bhikkhuni Sangha, an act viewed culturally as auspicious for her family and a life choice displaying "filial piety" with a decidedly different future from prostitution. Young girls, living together under the direction of senior female preceptors *(pavattini)*, not having to answer to monks (often leading to sexual abuse and scandals in the past), could gain direct experience of independent women's lives. As novices (*samaneri* or *bhikkhuni*), they would receive literacy training and learn practices of personal study that would remain transferable skills. Given Thai Buddhist custom, they could continue their adult lives in ecclesiastical work as spiritual leaders and service workers, or they could disrobe and use their skills for secular paid work, or become educated wives and mothers, modeling very different female identities to the larger society.

For this option to succeed in working toward gender justice in Thailand, Tavivat points out that the nuns must be independent of the traditional domination of monks. And that will require changed public policy, the establishment of new religious foundations, and a new politics of religious culture in that country. Inspiration for the struggle can be found in the flourishing of Buddhist nuns in post-World War II Taiwan. Today in that country, some of the most highly regarded universities, hospitals, charity organizations, and relief agencies have been established, administered, and funded by various orders of Buddhist nuns. Many of the women have become nuns after attaining advanced educations or after years of successful careers, seeing in their life choice a different option from the traditional Confucian "good mother, obedient wife."

The tragedy of AIDS in Thailand today, which has organized our discussion in this chapter, can be viewed as a collection and final result of multiple moral failures of individual families; or the corruption of individual police, military, and government officials; or the invasion into individual consciousnesses and subsequent conversions to a foreign and tragically flawed new religion. All are true. But putting the blame on individuals leads to nonsystemic responses. The tragedy should be viewed and responded to structurally. For that to happen, analyses of both local and global power and policies that address that power are required.

Institutional change is required, but such change is unavoidably controversial and political. Change must be local in terms of what works within a given culture—for example, the revival of the Bhikkhuni Sangha in Thailand. But change also requires the strengthening of international ties between women (and the men who work alongside them), who in their nations of origin face both different but related challenges. Gender justice in countries where most of the poorest of the poor are women and their children requires help from women and men of industrialized nations. We must use our power—our education, our critical skills, our organizing ability, our money, our connections, our life choices, and our careers—to work for structural changes that serve gender justice in a world where all issues of justice have become inextricably global.

World religions offer cross-cultural and cross-national connections that can help in that needed collaboration. So also, traditional religions offer significant subversive insights and resources to unveil, analyze, and combat the hopeless hope, the endlessly unsatisfying satisfactions, of the astonishingly successful new religion that is the religion of the market. In that religion, women find their value reduced to the status of a commodity, a process that in its own way makes prostitutes of us all, wearing signs that say "for sale" on our souls.

6. African Traditional Religions

AFRICA IS THE SECOND LARGEST CONTINENT ON THE PLANET. It comprises twenty-two percent of the Earth's land surface. However, it is far less densely populated than most places on planet Earth. For example, more people live in India today than live in all of Africa, although India has only one-tenth the landmass. If we confine our attention to sub-Saharan Africa (so-called Black Africa), the statistics on religious association, while only approximations, indicate a three-way tie: one-third Muslim, one-third Christian, and one-third traditional religions. Still, in most places in Africa it is by way of local languages that children first learn to name the world and define its reality. These indigenous languages are shaped and framed by the worldview and ethos of African traditional religions. This means that Africans who are Muslim and Africans who are Christian remain Africans, not Euro-Americans and not Middle-Eastern Arabs. In turning to these traditional belief systems and gender practices, we are looking at the peoples of Africa whose continuing cultures are firmly grounded in indigenous languages and passed between generations through proverbs and folklore.

Most Africans are born and raised in villages, although for the same reasons as elsewhere there is a recent movement toward urbanization. Today, the world of the village is the first world most African children learn. That was certainly the case with Mutombo Nkulu-N'Sengha, our guide for this chapter. There were no cultural imperatives for Mutombo's father to take only one wife. Both mother and father were children of chiefs in the ancient Luba empire of the central Congo, and polygamy remained a common practice among the Baluba people in the 1950s. Moreover, his father's decision stood in stark contrast to other lessons being taught by his village culture where, as Mutombo recalls, "the beating of wives was pretty much part of daily life, and some uncles practiced polygamy."

That village culture, like traditional religions in general, was oral, not text based. It is a culture that "writes" itself into memory by way of proverbs, folktales, religious ritual, and dance. It is also a culture and a religion that, however otherwise diverse, is everywhere patriarchal. This pervasive reality is inscribed in the lore of traditional proverbs that are passed from one generation to the next. Listening to these proverbs, we hear males talking to other males *about women*, replicating in oral culture the fear and disrespect found in the sacred writings of text-oriented religions. Here are some examples:

- "To marry is to put a snake in one's hand bag."
- "If a woman climbs a tree while she is menstruating, it will die."
- A Haussa proverb says *Kworvia tagari tana ragaya* ("A good woman stays home").
- Mothers and grandmothers tell young women, "If you do not cook you will not get a husband," while fathers tell their sons, "The more you help your wife [in domestic work], the more she gets lazy."
- "If you do not beat your wife, she will think you have a mistress."

Not just proverbs invest village life and consciousness with the socially constructed injustices of gender; common practices teach girls and boys their very different places in society. Women who are menstruating are forbidden to cook for their husbands and must spend their nights in a separate hut. Girls are expected to be virgins when marrying, while virginity in young men is "unmanly." Adultery is gendered with differing permissions and prohibitions, resulting in intra-family, male-to-female transfer as the most likely means for AIDS transmission. In Kinshasa (a major language of Central Africa) it is said by men to other men, *Kudia usuan Kudia maki* ("to eat the chick and the eggs"). It concerns a man having sex with both mother and daughter, an accomplishment that yields male bragging rights.

This pervasive background of gender bias and misogyny is reflected in a recent survey conducted in Nigeria that asked, "If you could be born again, would you choose to be a man or woman?" The response showed that 48 percent of the girls wanted to be born as boys, while only 6 percent of the boys wanted to be born as girls. What we find in Africa, in short, is no different from what we find in India or Thailand or Pakistan or Brazil or wherever—we find women oppressed by tradition, women silenced in tradition, and women excluded as polluted from ritual practices. This discrimination stands in marked contrast to other resources embedded in the indigenous culture that are remarkably free of gender bias.

Mutombo points out that traditional societies in Africa opened the door to female rulers, priestesses, and even army commanders. Concerning the voice of women, he claims to find not a closed but an open system, where the female voice makes a space for itself despite male oppression. We find the voice inside the construction of language. Thus, Bantu languages make no distinction between the pronouns "he" and "she." When women marry in Africa, they do not change their names to that of their husbands. In the Kiluba language the verb "to have" is replaced by the verb "to be with"; no man can say "I have a wife," but says instead, *Ndi ne mukaji* ("I am with a wife"). Given the centrality of ancestor worship in the social construction of authority, when speaking about both God and ancestors the words spill over gender boundaries. The Yoruba speak of God as "Mother." And in many tribes the myths of the ancestors disclose a male ancestor returning as a girl, or a woman ancestor reappearing as a boy. In African creation myths, women are created directly, not through a man. And in some myths she is born quite a while before man; many important things happen before "he" arrives.

More often than not, however, African religions speak of God neither as "he" nor "she," "mother" or "father," but in terms of transcendent mystery. The Baluba say that God is like *Malango* ("the thought") or *Luvula* ("the wind"). In Nigeria God is called *Ama-Anasi* ("the One known yet never fully known"). A Pygmy hymn asks:

Who can make an image of God?
He has no body.
He is as a word which comes out of your mouth.
That word. . . . It is no more,
It is past, and still it lives.

In traditional African religions, language about God offers no traction for those who would inscribe the transcendent with the male voice and figure.

But even more important, Mutombo claims, is the way African religions speak about the human. Even as speech about God transcends gender, so speech about the origin of males and females is absorbed and disappears into an inclusive and comprehensive language of fundamental personhood (*Bumuntu* in Central Africa, *Ubuntu* in South Africa, and *Eniyan* or *Iwapele* in West Africa). An Akan proverb from Ghana states, *Nnipa nyinaaz ye Onyame mona obi nnye asase ba* ("All human beings are children of God; no one is a child of this earth"). For the Baluba, each person is *Bana be Vidye Mukulu* ("a child of the Great Spirit").

With Mutombo's help, we will examine in more detail the views of this "human nature" as spoken by the Yoruba in West Africa and by the Baluba in Central Africa. In general in African religions, the origin of each person is seen to lie in the mystery and intention of the Divine; this belief is especially explicit with the Yoruba. In the creation myth of the Ifa, the construction of each person is viewed as a process of successive steps. First *Ara* ("the body") is given by *Orisa-ula*, the divine "crafter of the body." Then *Olodumare*, the Supreme Being, supplies the lifeless body with *Emi* ("spirit"). The now-animated body then travels to the house of *Ajala* (the "potter of heads") to choose an *Ori* (the bearer of individuation or personality but also of destiny). It is a choice made without benefit of foreknowledge but a choice that sets each person's life course. This idea speaks to the mystery of identity, a mystery standing behind the arbitrariness of the particularities of our birth (including gender but also ethnicity, the social location of one's family, one's place in the order of births, and so on). It is a fact that our parents chose or consented to have a child, but they did not and could not will us *as our self*. For the Yoruba, in this special sense each of us is "a child of God," who is nevertheless responsible to develop and perfect (or misuse and waste) what is put into our hands at birth.

While the *Emi* (the divine spirit) is the same and equal in all *Eniyan* (human beings), the Yoruba see in the *Ori* something that is at the same moment both divine and intimately personal. The *Ori* is each person's destiny/responsibility/character/personal guardian. It is spoken of as a "partner" or "double" and is viewed as a representation in each person of one of the 401 *Orisha* of the Yoruba pantheon.

While a person who misbehaves is spoken of as having no *opolo* ("brain"), it is the *Okan* or "heart" that the Yoruba see as the source and bearer of *Iwa,* character. Western social sciences have no place for such words as "heart" or "spirit." Still, in our society everyone knows what we mean when we say, "she has heart" or "he's got spirit." In everyday English, the word "heart" indicates a complexity of positive endowments—courage that is not a rough courage, but one that shows compassion. "Heart" connotes a life force, a determination that is not individualistic or autonomous but is positively connected to others. There is no other word in the English language that designates this complexity of character. We use such words routinely and know that what we have designated with such words are crucial qualities of character. Modern social science shows its own methodological limits by not being able to say, and thus not knowing how to think about, what "heart" is or what "spirit" is.

By way of contrast, words like "spirit" or "heart" or "beauty" (of character) are central to the African traditional religions and to their view of human personality. Character *(Iwa)* can be good *(Iwa rere)* or gentle *(Iwa pele).* Moreover, character is not something finished; it is something that is put into our hands at birth. As an Ifa proverb says, *Owo ara eni, Laafi I tunwa ara enii se* ("each individual must use his own hands to improve on his own character"). Our personal responsibility to grow or cultivate our "beauty" *(buya)* and our "good heart" *(Mucima muyampe)* is spoken of in this Luba proverb: *Vidye wa kuha buya nobe we mukwashako* ("God gave you beauty and goodness, but you must help him"). The Baluba speak of a *Muntu* (a person with good character) as distinguished from a *Kintu* (a person who has become a "thing"). It is believed that a human being can increase or deplete and lose his/her humanness. Thus, it is a widespread belief in Africa that people of bad character are not truly human. For example, the Yoruba of West Africa say *Ga se Motho* ("he is not human"), while the Baluba of Central Africa say *I mufu unanga* ("he is a dead body walking"). These are all claims made by Africans concerning fundamental anthropology that find no equivalents in the language or concepts of modern social science, and they show where that science fails to describe reality accurately.

It is important to recognize that in all this talk about character, about what it means to be human or to deplete and lose that humanness, the language used by Africans displays no gender bias. For example for the Yoruba, *Okan* (heart), *Emi* (spirit), and *Ori* (destiny/responsibility/character/ personal guardian) are the fundamentals out of which the human is constructed, and they are genderless. These ontological claims contradict the popular proverbs and cultural practices that demean and disgrace women. Indeed, they are positive resources that can be tapped to reverse the discourse of misogyny and to bring condemnation and ridicule upon those who speak and act with disrespect toward women.

We find these same positive resources in the ontological speculations of the Baluba people of Central Africa. Like the Yoruba, the Baluba also speak of a good person as *Munt wa mucinma muyampe* ("the person with a good heart"). The Baluba use the same word *buya* for both goodness and beauty. What makes a good person good is not so much obedience to law as gracefulness of living, an elegance and responsiveness in being with others that display ease and elicit harmony. A Luba proverb says, *Bwino bonso ke bwino, bwino i Kwikala hiya ne Bantu* ("the morally superior man/woman has learned the art of knowing how to live harmoniously with fellow human beings").

The "good heart" for the Baluba includes virtues such as *Llusa* (compassion), *Buswe* (love), *Buntu* (generosity), *Boloke* (honesty, integrity, fairness), *Butundaile* (hospitality), *Buleme* (respect, politeness), and *Bukwashi* (helpfulness). On the other hand, *mucima mubi* (the evil heart) displays *Bubela* (falsity), *Mushikwa* or *Nshikani* (hate), *Kibengo* (arrogance, insolence), and *Bunzazangi* (hypocrisy). These virtues and vices describe how one lives with others. Like the heart that connects us to others, they are elements of an ethic of the in-between, an ethic of connectedness. The virtues are gentle ones that nourish relationships. Indeed, the Luba name for the Supreme Being, *Leza*, is derived from the verb "to cherish." The will of the Supreme Being corresponds to the intention of the ancestors—to preserve, to nourish, and to cause to flourish.

This language reflects what we in the West might call "the feminine virtues"—the arts of showing and giving care. The graceful reception and hosting of others, knowing how to make people feel comfortable and at ease, feeling cared for and helped—for the

Baluba these constitute the *Bumuntu* (the essence of the genuinely human) and keep us harmoniously related to the way of the living universe, to the spirit of *Leza*, to "cherishing." As we humans are embraced and nourished by the world around us, upon which we remain so dependent, we need to show gratitude in our way of living with each other.

This African way of thinking about the good person and the good way of life is a powerful and positive resource to combat sexism and misogyny, that dis-ease that reflects male fear and contempt of the gender other, fear and contempt for relatedness and dependence, flight from and forgetfulness of all that nurtures. From the place that novelist Joseph Conrad called the "heart of darkness," from West and Central Africa, comes much light concerning the ways of the heart.

But how are we to apply these moral insights to the conditions of modern Africa and to the lives of women living under those conditions? Gender justice requires that we have our feet on the ground and show *Mwendelo muyampe*, "a good way of walking."

If you are a woman, it is not easy to walk well in Africa today. The vast majority of women are poor. Many of them are sick and getting sicker. Many of them are victims, as are their children, of those so-called masculine virtues of glory in war, in vendetta, and in revenge. Without structural change in the global political economy, Mutombo claims, things will only get worse. The well-being of women and the children they cherish and try to nurture is directly related to such basic things as clean water, adequate food and sanitation, and men who are engaged with women in making a life together rather than in making war. Unfortunately, in Africa today these are in short supply. And that, Mutombo argues, is not accidental or bad luck.

Joseph Conrad wrote his novel *Heart of Darkness* between 1889 and 1899, when global capitalism was becoming engaged in the "scramble" for Africa. It was an era marked as well by the onset of the automobile and its bottomless thirst for rubber for tires. The Congo that Conrad wrote about was a prime source for that commodity. In 1900 the population of the Congo basin was estimated at 20 million. An official census taken in 1911 showed that only 8.5 million were still alive. The African proverb "the white man's work eats people" refers to conditions on those rubber plantations. One hundred years later, that work that "eats people" continues.

Today, it is not rubber in the Congo but diamonds and copper; local warlords act both as an occupying force and as go-betweens for global entrepreneurs in Amsterdam, Brussels, and London. Behind the ethnic hatred, and fanning those flames, are the old colonial tactics of "divide and rule." And the weapons with which those misnamed "tribal wars" are fought are the weapons left behind by the Cold War, weapons grown cold and silent in Europe but not in Africa, where they remain "guns for hire" and hot from action.

An even more lethal weapon—and one aimed especially at women—is the AIDS virus. We may think of this disease as linked primarily to individual moral failure, or perhaps to a cultural moral failure that condones sexual permissiveness. However, such an angle of vision fails to consider the geography of the contagion's spread in Africa. It spread along the major truck routes that carried out raw materials desired by the industrial North. And it was not just truck drivers who spread the disease, but a new culture of conspicuous consumption that traveled back up the highways that the raw materials were traveling down. An enormously seductive culture beckoned the young from their families and villages and introduced them to the life of urban glitter and excitement. But for the uneducated and young (half of the world's population today is under twenty-five, and more than half of those youth live in Africa), the jobs in the city could not deliver on the dreams held out in advertisements and movies. Something structural—both in the global political economy and in the global politics of culture— dislodged consciences that once embraced traditional values. First the heart and the spirit became infected with conspicuous consumption; only later the body contracted AIDS.

To these more recent assaults of war and disease upon women, we must add the ancient scourge of poverty. According to a report by the World Bank, between 1990 and 2000 the number of people living in poverty in sub-Saharan Africa rose by 85 million to a total of 265 million. This same period saw 30 percent of the world's poor living in Africa, up from 16 percent in 1985. Clearly, what we call development has had its winners and its losers; overwhelmingly, the losers are poor women and their children in the two-thirds world. Although they comprise half the world's population, women constitute 70 percent of the poor, with two-thirds of them never having been taught to read or write.

Once again, Mutombo would warn us away from conceiving poverty as an accident of history and geography—bad luck at the great lottery wheel of conception. For example, part of the global political economy is the politics of global debt. In the same years poverty was increasing in Africa, so was foreign debt—totaling $272 billion in 1990, almost double what it was just ten years before. The rules governing world markets and trade mean that poor countries lose at least $500 billion to the rich countries each year, which is ten times as much as they receive in aid. Add to this the fact that in most nations of sub-Saharan Africa the level of debt (interest and payments due) surpasses their annual gross national product.

What does gender justice require of us—especially if that "us" is we who are presently reading this book and are therefore both literate and educated? First, it obliges us to study, to learn the facts, to become practiced in the art of critical thinking. We must engage in the kind of analysis that does not stop at the surface or appearance of things, but goes behind the images we see on the television news to the structural realities of a global political economy. For the poor of Africa and elsewhere, economic development often translates into "the work that eats people." We should feel sorry for the flood victims and send them aid. But we should also examine the practices of clear-cutting forests to maximize profits, leaving the ground hard that once absorbed monsoon rains and prevented floods. The desertification that is spreading south from the Sahara and causing famine as it spreads should not be seen as a "tragedy of nature," but as a predictable result of the farming methods introduced by global agribusiness. Let us follow the story of food a bit further. It seems uniquely appropriate when talking about the well-being of women and their children. Food—its planting and harvesting, its distribution and marketing, its preparation and serving—remains the great work of our species.

We have already talked about food and money and how the logic of global agriculture is increasingly shaped and formed by the logic of profits. One result is that the price of rice goes up in places like northern Thailand even as the price of winter vegetables in Tokyo becomes more competitive and cheap. Development theorists did not intend this to happen. Agricultural science sought to develop new seeds for rice and corn and soy beans—the staple foods of most of the world's peoples—in order to end starvation. The manipulation of the DNA of the seeds to produce larger yields was announced in the 1950s as "the green revolution" that would end world hunger. These were, indeed, "miracle seeds"—but some of the miracles they produced were unintended. The new seeds needed pesticides and fertilizers; in dry land areas like much of Africa close to the Sahara, they needed irrigation and deep wells and pumps. In other words, the new seeds needed money. As a result, the genetic code of the altered seeds revolutionized the face of agriculture around the world. Everywhere it has meant the displacement of peasant subsistence farmers by landlords who have capital—often the landlords are gigantic foreign corporations. And everywhere in the world land has become dependent upon artificial fertilizers while the aquifers become depleted. We are ruining the land and running out of water.

The well-meaning scientists who designed those new seeds did not foresee that food is political. Food involves the most basic of everyday needs and dependencies. It employs far more human workers in its cultivation, its transportation, its merchandising, and its preparation than any other human work. Of course, a sizeable portion of that work is work done by women without pay. Food is power in people's lives, and food once drawn into the global monetary system is profits. Food is political.

In Africa, peasant subsistence farmers have been displaced from their land. They have become seasonal day laborers on huge plantation farms, working for those who have the capital the new seeds require. Or they or their children have moved to the cities looking for paid work they cannot find in the countryside. That is a displacement not only of work but, more importantly, of the geography of conscience and of moral formation. It is, as I have suggested, not unconnected to the spread of AIDS. The irony and the tragedy are that seeds meant to feed the world's poor beckoned entrepreneurs looking for profits into areas that had been left to subsistence farming—unavailable for profits and therefore uninteresting to those seeking new sources of profit. As in earlier colonial times the missionaries were soon followed by businessmen, so in new colonial times international agribusiness soon followed the well-meaning agronomists. Not only did ownership of land and the style of cultivation change (often draining down precipitously the deep aquifers that sustain water tables around the world), but new crops were introduced, not the rice and corn originally intended. In northern Africa the same thing happened as in northern Thailand. Winter fruits and vegetables for sale in Europe replaced the cultivation of local staple crops. Staple, subsistence food slowly became more expensive as demand remained the same while supply diminished. Food provides an excellent example of how profit-driven "development" is making the rich richer and the poor poorer. And as I have said again and again, women and their children make up the vast majority of the poor, everywhere in the world.

What are we to do?

The Yoruba of West Africa say *Iwa lesin* ("good character is the essence of religion"). The traditional religions of Africa have much to teach us about gender and justice and about *Mucima muyampe*—the "good heart." But "good hearts" are not enough. Poor women everywhere need better science, more politically sophisticated science, and politically active support from concerned people in industrialized countries. Supporters must be knowledgeable in the politics of food, in the politics of water, in the politics of health care (nowhere in Africa does the health system offer AZT or protease inhibitors to those infected with HIV/AIDS), in the politics of "who runs things" and who benefits.

And that is where we come in—we who are educated, we who can think how the world works and see it critically, we who are lucky enough to have knowledge and access to new information. Yes, here at the end of this chapter we leave Africa behind. We are not there; we are here. Morally, we are obliged to return to where we are, which is where the power is, where decisions are made, and where responsibility rests.

7. Taoism

To read the *Lao-Tzu* is to realize that you have entered a discourse on gender. And it is a discourse that so obviously privileges counter-masculinist values that you are forced to conclude that the intentions of the author(s) were consciously subversive. (Scholars debate whether "Lao-Tzu" refers to a single author or to a literary genre of wise sayings. I have chosen to use the term in its generic sense.) Indeed, one way to read the *Lao-Tzu* is as a politics of reversal, a politics not of force but of the soft and of the gentle. It is a political philosophy presented as an ontology. In the five thousand-character text, "softness" is mentioned eleven times and "weakness" (understood as strength) ten times. Concerning what is really real in life, the *Lao-Tzu* teaches: "The weak and the tender overcome the hard and the strong" (chap. 36). And, "keeping to weakness is called strength" (chap. 5).

> In the whole world, nothing is softer and weaker than water. And yet for attacking the hard and the strong, nothing is better. There is nothing you can use to replace it. That the weak can overcome the strong—that the soft can overcome the hard—there is no one in the whole world who doesn't know it, and yet there is no one who puts it into practice. (chap. 78)

Literally, *Tao* means "the way" and *Te* means both "power" and "virtue." In chapter 51 we read:

> Tao gives birth to them and Te nourishes them; substance gives them form and their unique capacities complete them. Therefore the ten thousand things (of pluriform life) venerate Tao and honor Te. . . . (Tao) gives birth to all beings but doesn't try to own them. It acts on all beings but doesn't make them dependent; it matures them but doesn't rule them.

And, lest we miss the point, in the chapter immediately following we find: "The world had a beginning, which can be considered the *mother* of the world, in order to understand her children.

Having understood the children, if you return and hold on to the *mother*, till the end of your life you'll suffer no harm." Or again in chapter 34:

> The Great Tao flows everywhere. It may go left or right. All things depend on it for life, and it does not turn away from them. It accomplishes its task, but does not claim credit for it. It clothes and feeds all things but does not claim to be master over them. Always without desires, it may be called The Small. All things come to it, and it does not master them. It may be called The Great. Therefore (the sage) never strives himself for the great, and thereby the great is achieved.

Taoism presents us with a subversive discourse, and what it subverts is patriarchy.

Our guide for the study of Taoism is Liu Xiaogan. About his early life growing up poor in China, he remembers that in a period of famine their prized chicken grew ill and died. Liu remembers how his mother, without telling anyone, cooked and tasted the chicken to see if it was safe to eat. Only the next morning, when she had not gotten ill, did she present the chicken to the family to eat. Liu learned the meaning of "mother" from his own mother, a meaning he finds echoing throughout Taoism.

It is Xiaogan's contention that the *Lao-Tzu* constructed its ontology as a conscious critique of the way of power and privilege as displayed in the Confucianism of the time. (Scholars date the appearance of the *Lao-Tzu* to the period of the Warring States, 402–222 B.C.E.) Liu argues, for example, that the *Lao-Tzu* builds a metaphysics that is diametrically opposed to the notion that the universe is created by a single "God" who then "rules" or "governs." The language of authorship and of origin, and therefore of ownership and control, is an obvious discourse of legitimation. What it legitimates is the politics of hierarchy and patriarchy—a politics of top-down power. And that Confucian way of rule offended the *Lao-Tzu*'s sense of how the universe actually works. What, then, is that way? What is Tao?

Tao is not a being (God, for example). Indeed, it is closer to nonbeing (pure potentiality) than to being—understood as plural actualities or beings. Tao is invisible, inaudible, subtle, formless, and infinite. No word can grasp or name it: "There is something nebulous existing, born before heaven and earth, silent, empty, standing alone, altering in no way. Moving cyclically without becoming exhausted, which may be called *mother* of all under heaven. I know not its name. I give its alias, Tao" (chap. 25; emphasis added). The reader should note that this has a veiled but powerful political message. Before there is heaven there is already the really real (called "mother"), and it gives no mandate—an idea that strikes at the very heart of the Confucian pretension that sustains the notion of political legitimacy.

The root, the source, the breathing of the universe is not like a monarch, nor is it like a court and its bureaucracy (with angels and saints and intermediaries and go-betweens). Tao is something present without self-presentation, something that gives birth without trying to possess—"it acts on all beings but doesn't make them dependent, it matures them but doesn't rule them." Tao is feminine: "The spirit of the valley never dies. This is called the mysterious femininity (*xuan pin* or *hsiuan-pin*). The gateway of the mysterious femininity is called the root of heaven and earth. It continues on as if ever present. And in its use, it is inexhaustible" (chap. 6). Or again, "When you know masculine yet hold on to femininity, you'll be the ravine of the country. When you're the ravine of the country, your constant virtue will not leave. And when your constant virtue doesn't leave, you'll return to the state of the infant" (chap. 28). Tao is mother. Fundamental ontology is feminine. And so is fundamental axiology.

In chapter 25 we find this moral instruction: "Human persons model themselves on the Earth; the Earth models itself on Heaven; Heaven models itself on Tao." Let us think more carefully about this idea of humans modeling ourselves "on the earth." We have noted before that, for a number of world religions, the Earth, like the human body, is something to be despised, something from which, through rigorous spiritual discipline, men (and a few women) can escape. But not for Taoism! We are to look upon the Earth as an infant looks upon her mother. We are to regard Earth, learn from Earth, and model ourselves on what we learn.

Following that instruction, if we think carefully about Earth, about body and materiality, we will eventually realize that each of us has *two bodies,* although we almost always think we have only one—namely, our inside-the-skin body. This "in here" body is a body that separates and distinguishes. It is a body that makes some male and others female, a body that makes some of us black and some of us white, a body that particularizes us in time and space (the thus-and-so of personal destiny). We take hold of our inside-the-skin body because it seems to let us hold onto our place in life for a while.

But we have another body—just as intimate to us and just as necessary. It is our outside-the-skin body, a body we share with all living things. It is a body that is constantly giving herself to us. We breathe. We drink water. Our body weight is 70 percent water. We constantly wash ourselves in nature's watery embrace, cleansing ourselves with gifts from the Earth. We mistakenly think that the purpose of our inside-the-skin body is to keep the outside out, to keep us from "spilling out" or "getting polluted." In fact, its purpose is to let the outside in—air, water, food, sight, touch, smell, hearing—our inside-the-skin body is forever busy letting the outside in. As Taoism teaches us, we live embraced by Tao, embraced by the mothering that gives birth to us at each moment of our lives.

Unlike our inside-the-skin body, our outside body does not separate us but instead unites us—not just to other humans but to all living things and to that which keeps all life here on Earth alive. More. When our inside-the-skin body dies, our other body continues. As the *Lao-Tzu* puts it: "A leaf when it falls, falls close to its root." In death we return to the place we have never left and a place that has never left us. We are never abandoned; we are never alone. We are embraced in life and in death by Tao.

Our outside-the-skin body (Tao) is a body that is present without demanding recognition, our constant benefactor without asking for notice, always giving without grasping. Such a notion of the really real implies a very different sense of the appropriate, of what is practical and thus should be practiced. How distant this is from the self-interested notion of self, so popular in economics, and the idea of a world that is best organized as a market. Also, how distant Tao (the Way) is from "the will to power" (of Nietzsche or of Freud or of Saint Augustine). Unfortunately, the politics of free markets and the power state govern our world today. And this, we are taught, is the way of hardheaded wisdom and truth. For the

Lao-Tzu, however, "the city of this Earth" teaches us a different wisdom, the arts of a generous hosting. We humans and other-than-human living things are treated as guests. And just as a good host is never intrusive, so we know Tao is present by her seeming absence. She "acts on all beings but doesn't make them dependent, [she] matures them but doesn't rule them."

If philosophy is politics that has not yet discovered itself or that has already forgotten itself, then Taoism, at least in its initial phase, does not suffer from this forgetfulness. It is a metaphysics that has politics constantly in mind. Like a good host, like Tao, the best rulers rule without being noticed or wanting to be noticed. In chapter 17, we find this statement: "The best rulers are those whose existence is merely known by the people; the next best are those who are loved and praised. The next are those who are feared. And the next are those who are reviled. . . . [The great ruler] accomplishes his task and completes his work and thus the people say he is natural." According to Liu, this is a conscious contrast to the Confucian idea of political rule, where the "good" ruler is always loved and revered, the bad ruler at least feared, but no ruler should ever be "merely known." Taoism, by contrast, finds a surer sign of wisdom in humor, in a kind of self-mocking. "He who feels pricked," they say, "must once have been a bubble."

The claim that has guided my reading of Taoism thus far is that it presents us with a political philosophy in the guise of an ontology. And it is an ontology and a politics consciously gendered. This gendering of ultimate reality is most popularly presented in the West in terms of the Taoist double-fish-sign, the *yin* and *yang.*

The figure is usually misunderstood as presenting in figure form the complementarities of male and female. But it is more accurately understood in terms of "reversion" or "reversal" *(fan).* Yin and *yang* are dynamic and ever changing. The relationship is less a fixed complementarity than a dialectic, and it is a dialectic in which the "weak" turns out to be the "strong." *Yin* and *yang* can be translated female and male, but also soft and hard, or wet and dry, or dark and bright, or—most significant of all—nonbeing and being. And here is the reversal: For the *Lao-tzu* it is the quietness, the "inactivity" of nonbeing that holds the superior position. It is that unformed, pure potential that is the source and ground of all particular actualities or beings. That which has position, that which stands out, asserts itself, and takes action—that which seems powerful—is reversed. Instead, the high becomes low and, like water against a rock, the subtle and the weak overcomes the hard and the strong.

This picture of the Way of ultimate reality is at the same moment a picturing to us of a way of human living that reflects this larger picture, a way of life that is "fitting." Nonassertiveness, taking "no action" *(wuwei)* or, better yet, being "spontaneous" *(ziran)* is what is valued as appropriate. And spontaneity needs no training. It is a wisdom that is the opposite of credentialed and specialized knowledge.

A later Taoist scholar (or school of scholarship), the *Chuang Tzu*, took these ideas of "reversal" *(fan)* and of the fitting and applied them to epistemology, naming it "no knowledge" or "ignorance." All knowledge, the *Chuang Tzu* argues, is perspectival, a seeing of things from a certain point of view (among many possible points of view). Every perspective is relative to its opposite. Official knowledge, knowledge that is credentialed (and is credentialing!) tries to establish its place, assert its position, and prove its point of view. (We should be aware how entrance into the Confucian bureaucratic hierarchy depended upon training in specialized knowledge and performance on exams.) But the price such knowing pays is an arrogance that thinks of itself as learned, a seeing that does not see the unseen in its seeing, does not see that all seeing is political, and refuses to acknowledge its own relationship to power, the bias of its own perspective.

This sounds remarkably like postmodern critical thought and someone like Michel Foucault, who claims to do to knowledge what knowledge does to what it knows—to subject it. Thus, Foucault is uninterested in the *what* of what is known but rather in *how* it comes to be known as knowledge—how it is manufactured,

how it is produced and distributed, how it guilds itself and monop-
olizes the market (much as university departments do), how it creates new needs and new markets, which groups benefit from such
knowledge, and which groups get subjected by it. In light of the
information age and the knowledge economy, Taoism would
instruct us to be suspicious of that knowledge, suspicious of its pretension, suspicious of its complicity with power, suspicious of its
ambition to take hold of the world in order to run it.

For Taoism the opposite of such knowledge is the wisdom of
"no-knowledge." It is a sensibility that is open, inquisitive, unpre-
tentious, and therefore unpretending. And it yields a way of action
that is subtle and spontaneous *(ziran)*, attentive and responsive to
context. But it is spontaneous not as naïveté or ineptitude but as
excellence of craft or art, a doing of what is gracious and graceful.
Neither portentous nor pretentious, the truly skilled for Taoism are
the quietly gifted. They are like a mother knowing, without having
to stop to think about it, what to do when hearing a baby cry.

What we find in the *Lao-Tzu* is a whole worldview, a whole
ethos—a whole religion—presented to us as feminine. It demands
of us that we think through reality from an entirely new perspective. What we have is mother instead of father, reality as birth
instead of creation, letting be instead of taking charge, spontaneity
instead of obedience and submission. It is difficult to conceive of a
more challenging presentation of ultimate reality or a more positive resource in world religions for talking about justice in gender
relations and why that justice is fitting and appropriate.

We are left with an obvious question, along with an answer that
is also obvious: Why are these positive resources absent from subsequent discourses on gender in China? Not only did Confucianism
win, Taoism itself became transformed. As emperors took on Confucian ways, disillusioned Taoist intellectuals became practiced at
the arts of withdrawal from politics, of avoiding contamination in
the always-limited field of the possible. As intellectuals retreated
into a kind of aristocracy of the disappointed soul, Taoism as a
practice became increasingly a religion just like other religions—
marketing religious capital, monopolizing the field of salvation.

As Taoism developed into a self-sustaining and professionalized
religion, in place of the natural, of the "not-knowing," we find
instead an esoteric knowledge, a magic and alchemy of imagined

body chemistry. Religious Taoism became a set of specialized and guilded practices fixated on power—the power to gain adherents by claiming to demonstrate the power to protect against illnesses and endure diseases, the power to unlock the secret powers of longevity even unto immortality. At the same time, institutionally, Taoism became a male gerontocracy—old male alchemists and old male mystics and old male ascetics living alone in caves. And with that transformation, all the silliness about women and women's bodies and sexuality returned! Among the otherwise interesting Taoist "arts of the bedchamber," we find that the art of arts, the master art, is the art of conserving semen. We find a disciplined rejection of ejaculation, the holding onto and hoarding up of the male life force, while the female genitalia are viewed as a place of test and danger, of possible loss, of exhaustion, and of eventual death. Taoism is certainly not alone in such foolishness. But neither does it in the end depart from such misogyny.

After a most promising beginning—promising in terms of gender and gender justice, Taoism becomes the opposite of Tao, a contradiction of naturalness. The politics of gender reversal have become again the same old politics of patriarchal fear that approaches women with suspicion and control. What began with mother and with birth ends up pictured as the heaven of the immortals, a lonely mountain cave—a barren womb that needs no further birth because what is born but then perfected by religious practices is thought never to die. We arrive at the end with a being who no longer needs mother.

Let me close on a more positive note. In its earliest phase, Taoism was revolutionary in terms of its worldview and ethos. It presented the possibility of a quiet and gentle revolt:
- of the low against the high
- of the soft against the hard
- of the wise against the professionally learned
- of the giving against the grasping
- of letting be against taking charge
- of birth against creation

and the return to mother.

8. Native American Religions

WE TURN TO OUR FINAL CHAPTER. And as we do, we travel east across the Pacific just as sometime between thirty and sixty thousand years ago, when a land bridge stretched from Siberia to Alaska, the ancient ancestors of the North and South American Indian populations also traveled. That may be one reason for the remarkable similarity in worldview and ethos between Taoism and Native American religions. More likely still is the fact that both populations were deeply and daily dependent upon agriculture, fishing, and hunting and expressed their attachment and gratitude in their religious beliefs and rituals without any second thoughts about a God above and beyond it all.

Unlike Taoism, Native American religions have no founder(s), no written texts, no official clergy or formal religious institutions. Instead, there are folktales, aphorisms, and traditions of gifted orators. There are also dances, dreams, and, above all, visions. These elements allow an intense flexibility to adjust and respond to differences in locality and in everyday conditions of life.

Scholars divide Native American religions into two broad categories—the hunting tribes and the horticultural tribes—although the division is rough and the borders are porous. We shall concentrate upon the longhouse traditions of the Mohawk Nation, because it is to these peoples that our guide, Christopher Ronwanien:te Jocks, traces his origin. But first I will discuss some general features shared by all the religions of our country's First Nations peoples.

In the 1630s, Jesuit missionaries traveled into the area of the Great Lakes to offer Christian salvation to Indian peoples whose religious practices astonished the good fathers. One of them, Father Francois du Perron, wrote the following:

> All their actions are dictated to them directly by the devil, who speaks to them now in the form of a crow or some simi-

lar bird, now in the form of a flame or a ghost, and all this in dreams, to which they show great deference. They consider the dream as the master of their lives; it is the God of the country. It is this which dictates to them their feasts, their hunting, their fishing, their war, their trade with the French, their remedies, their dances, their games, their songs.

In this unfriendly quote, we find an accurate description of the religious ways of the Indian peoples. Dreams and visions are the primary means of communication with the divine, the Great Spirit, the Father God, and Mother Earth, and the primary means of mediation of the gift most sought, supernatural power, as displayed most potently in shamans and medicine men (and occasionally medicine women). Dreams and visions, together with the idea of cosmic harmony and the cycle of life and death, are religious attitudes found embedded everywhere in Native North American religious myths and rituals.

Concerning cosmic harmony, most Indian myths of origin trace back to a time of "first beginning" when all beings on earth were human. But a great change is said to have taken place, a time when the primal beings changed into animals and birds and only today's humans retained their original form. As a consequence, Native American religion retains a close connection between humans and other-than-human beings, a spiritual bond that makes the sharp division in most religions between humans and animals simply disappear—or not appear in the first place. All animals are thought to be endowed with spiritual force and must be approached, therefore, with the kind of respect and care you would show a human brother or sister. For example, all bears are held to be mysterious, and some bears are so powerful that they can talk or change forms (as experienced in dreams and visions). Stones are sometimes thought to be alive; medicine men and medicine women can talk to them and gain valuable knowledge. All of created reality is potentially spiritually potent, though most of the time it remains "secular" and safe. While our Western religions focus religious devotion upon a God who is separate from and transcends his creation, Native American spirituality holds that everyday life is confronted by and accompanied by an abundance of "spirits" and "powers." Trees, birds, fish, clouds, streams, the wind, the land—all are sacred and to be approached with gratitude.

Indeed, it is gratitude that is found everywhere among the Native peoples of North America, the most spiritually appropriate and accurate attitude, which both corresponds and responds to the living plenitude that is the really real that encompasses all. What lives also dies; however, death holds little interest in most Native religious myths because so little can be known about it. How astonishing the Mormons, with their elaborate geography of the afterlife, must have seemed to their Native American neighbors. There is some speculation in the religions of the First Nations concerning reincarnation, that death is not an end but part of a continuing cycle of death and rebirth seen everywhere in the seasonal patterns of nature. But such speculation receives little attention in either myth or ritual. For most Native Americans, the dead are gone and we will not see them again (although in spirit they may be in the wind that brushes through your hair). The mystery of death—its arbitrariness, its impenetrability—is posed powerfully in the myth of the origin of death as spoken by the Lepan Apache people. This is what they say:

> In the beginning of the world, when the animal people were created, when trees and grass and animals and birds were people, everything was going along well. It went along well until the middle of time. There was no death.
>
> They began to talk about it. Some said it would be best to have death. Others were against it. They talked about it. Many wanted to live forever.
>
> Raven was the one who said, "I want death to exist." The others said, "Well, if there must be death, let them die and we will put them away, but let them come back to life in four days."
>
> "No." said Raven. "I'll take this pebble and drop it in the water. If it floats there will be no death, but if it stays down, then there will be death. They will not come back to life in four days."
>
> So Raven dropped the stone in the water. It never rose to the surface.
>
> Then Raven said, "Well, you see that. When people die they cannot come back to life anymore."
>
> Raven was the very first one to lose a child. He said, "You people said that when anyone died he would come back to life in four days." The others answered, "No, you are the one

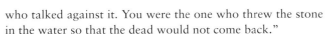

who talked against it. You were the one who threw the stone
in the water so that the dead would not come back."
Then Raven started to cry. He put his child away. After
that, people died.

The mystery of loss and grief is expressed but not resolved. When
we put our loved ones away, "they do not come back." But we may
hear their spirits laughing in the babble of water running over
rocks.

The spirituality of American First Nations peoples focuses upon
life here and now and not on the life to come. Its focus is on care
and on a sense of cultivated mutuality. Why cultivated? Because we
humans are part of the cosmic harmony and must do our part in
maintaining that harmony. This mutuality is most intensely experienced in relationship to our most fundamental dependency, in relationship to food. Religious myths and rituals having to do with
food, therefore, are central in the devotional life of Native Americans. We can see this in two ceremonies, one having to do with "the
master of animals" and the other the important seasonal ritual
called the Sun Dance with its worship of the Corn Maidens. Each
animal species has its own lord and master, usually conceived as an
animal spirit of awesome proportions. The giant beaver governs
the behavior of everyday beavers and allots them as food to human
hunters; it also guides the spirits of the dead animal in their return
to the world of the living. The same is true of fish and of game
birds, but especially of buffalo.

The picture in our heads of buffalo hunts with Indians majesti-
cally riding incredibly agile ponies is quite wrong. Horses were
introduced by the Spanish, and only in the sixteenth century.
Before that, the hunt was the far more precarious business of stalk-
ing and running, and the outcome both uncertain and essential.
This precarious dependence called forth powerful religious cere-
monials; Plains Indians imitated the movement of buffaloes in their
dancing, wearing buffalo horns and skins as acts of supplication. It
was not an "act of magic" as the missionaries supposed, but a form
of prayer, a way of beseeching the animal spirit to cooperate in the
hunt and offer itself to the kill.

The same is true of the Sun Dance, which Native Americans
thought of not as a magical manipulation of nature but as a grateful
participation in annual renewal. The Sun Dance reenacts creation

and its ongoing renewal—not only of animal and vegetable life here on Earth, but of the whole of cosmic evolution and harmony. With the departure of the Corn Maidens comes the withering away of vegetable food. Upon their happy return, a return implored and empowered through religious ritual, nature again waxes fertile and green.

Given the this-worldly pragmatism of Native American spirituality, it should come as no surprise that Mother Earth receives more devotional attention than Father God. In the Sun Dance, Mother Earth receives offerings of tobacco poured out on the ground. Indeed, whenever there is a communal feast, a bowl of water is brought and a portion poured out upon the ground—the sacred ground upon which we walk and from which we draw our life.

Still, Native Americans can be as self-contradictory in their religious attitudes as any other religious folks. Thus, in these central religious rituals the dancers are exclusively male. Women are permitted to observe, can even be members of the choir, but are excluded from the primary religious actions of the dance itself. Worse still, in venerating Mother Earth, First Nations religions demean the concrete human female body. Everywhere we find that old taboo about women and menstruation and pollution. At puberty, the boys becoming men are sent out alone or in the company of other boys into the forests or the mountains to suffer, to fast, and to face the dangers of predatory beasts. All this they do in quest of their personal vision, the goal of the vision quest that is reserved for boys and not girls. While it is true that a few women (not many) may become medicine women, their empowering vision quest can be undertaken only after menopause. As long as women are menstrual, they are considered impure and religiously dangerous. Not even Mother Earth is ritually accessible to adult women except by way of male mediation. Menstruation is thought to be like death in that both carry powerful taboo energy that can contaminate ritual, require careful supervision, and, in cases of violation (or suspected violation because of ritual failure), can result in public exposure and punishment.

Putting this aside, we will follow the guidance of Christopher Ronwanien:te Jocks, whose research on the Longhouse tradition tells a different story, one that reveals a once-powerful and empowering place for women among the Mohawk people of Upper New

York State and southern Quebec. "Longhouse," Chris tells us, refers to a matrilineal and multi-family structure in which the Mohawk people lived until the dismantling of that culture by the white man's conquest in the mid-eighteenth century. Today, "Longhouse" refers to people who seek to revive the prior ways and to the physical structures where they meet for public and ceremonial occasions.

Such occasions always begin with an opening, in Mohawk *ohon:ton karihwatehken* or the "Thanksgiving Address," a speech that takes listeners upon a journey through all of creation, with its multiple interdependencies. Time and again the speaker reiterates, "for this we express our thanks, and so our minds are together." Such communal remembrance and thanksgiving are the deep work of culture, work that Mohawk people find to fit the peculiar aptitude of women. Women, as the bearers and nurturers of children, are also recognized as the primary workers and bearers of culture.

Chris tells us that women's favored social position and their leadership roles are formalized in the Iroquois tradition. Iroquois women are the keepers and holders of three kinds of titles, including: (1) the title to land, (2) the clan name or titles that link every individual to their history and to each other, and (3) the fifty chiefs' titles that establish the Iroquois system of governance. Clan mothers had the duty and the right according to the "Great Law" (in Mohawk *Kaianeren'ko:wa*) to invest the chief (always a male) with his titles of office. In theory, this was a lifelong investment. But the Council of Clan Mothers retained the right to divest a chief deemed to be persistently abusive of his power. This supervisory authority of women as clan mothers was rooted, in turn, in traditional spiritual practices. Audrey Shenandoah, a contemporary Iroquois clan mother from the Onondaga people, points out:

> The clan mothers' duties have to do with the community affairs, the nation affairs, but they also have another role and that has to do with the spiritual side. They set ceremonial times and watch the moon for our people. We . . . still have those people who must watch the phases of the moon, who know when it is time to call the faith keepers and the women together to sit, and to set time for the ceremonies which are held at various times throughout the year.

This prominence of the female in the work of culture is given powerful mythic voice in a traditional narrative concerning the origin and first reception of the "Great Law." It is said that a woman, Tsikonhsahsen, was the first to accept the new way of life (of community and co-responsibility). The story continues. A lone male holdout, the feared cannibal Atotarho, resists the civilizing ways until the Peacemaker adds Tsikonhsahsen to those who "shall together form a circle, standing alongside your body." This is how the speech of the Peacemaker is remembered, and how the Great Law became established.

> "Now, moreover, it is accomplished;
> now she has arrived,
> our mother, the Great Matron whose name is Tsikonhsahsen;
> now she has accepted the Good Message,
> and this moreover is what you should confirm and adopt,
> the Great Law,
> so that she may place antlers on you, our mother,
> and they shall together form a circle, standing alongside your
> body."
> Thereupon the man [Atotarho] looked at Tekaihoken and
> Hayenhwatha'
> and Tsha'tekaihwate' and Ho'tatshehte' and Skanyataiyo' and
> Tsha'tekaenhyes.
> Thereupon Tekanawita said,
> "Now you are looking at all of the ones who will be standing
> with you."
> Thereupon the man bowed his head.
> Thereupon his hair stopped writhing and all of his fingers
> became quiet.
> Thereupon Tekanawita said,
> "Now, indeed, it is functioning, the Peace."

In a warrior society, with its memories of blood and destruction, women and mothers are recognized and remembered as the bearers of life instead of death, of law and of decency instead of the chaos of violence. Indian men are prepared by long discipline for the chase and the kill, prepared as warriors to die rather than to lose face, haunted by the knowledge of possible defeat and of the carnage that will come down like thunder upon the women and children waiting behind. But all this bravery and bravado is purposeless without that more ultimate reality, peace that alone allows life to thrive. Life—everyday life with its birthing, with its children laughing and crying, with food to be cooked and served—life that gives life across the generations, the warrior realizes, is the work of women. That is the hard-won truth of Native American cultures. They have learned that what men owe women and what women want from men, above all else, is peace.

Biographies

Anantanand Rambachan was born in Trinidad where his great-grandparents had moved to escape a famine in India. He remembers bitterly how his own mother, although of the Brahman class, was forced by Hindu tradition to drop out of a promising school career in order to marry. She was twelve years old! Anant received his graduate education at Leeds University in England, where he learned of Christian liberation theology and became persuaded that Hinduism must also develop liberating practices, especially on the issue of gender, or cease to be a relevant religious tradition. Today, he teaches at Saint Olaf College in Minnesota, where he reports that the women students continue to press him on the issue of "the silencing of women in Hindu sacred texts." Also, in 1987 his first child was born—a daughter.

Gerard S. Sloyan was born into a Roman Catholic family in New York City. The Catholic Church would educate both himself and two of his sisters to the doctoral level. One of his sisters became a mathematician and college president, while Gerry, teaching at Catholic University of America, played a leading role in the liturgical reforms of Vatican II. He became disappointed in the actual effects of that council regarding the rights of women in the life of the church. But he expects all that to change in the new century, the result of pressure not from the clergy but from the laity.

Marvin Ellison teaches Christian ethics at Bangor Theological Seminary in Maine. He grew up in the Old South just as the churches, especially the Black churches, went into rebellion against "the peculiar institution" of segregation and overthrew it. Marvin saw what the church could accomplish when dedicated to liberation. But as he grew older and became aware that his own sexual orientation was "different," he also learned how repressive the church has been and still is on matters of gender and sexuality. Still, at its best he says, "the church offers a kind of 'free zone' to experiment with freedom and try on this radical call to inclusivity and mutual well-being for all."

Our two Muslim guides, *Asghar Ali Engineer* of India and *Farid Esack* of South Africa, represent the diversity of Islamic peoples and their readiness to consider fundamental change in the religious attitude toward women. Asghar has had to survive five assassination attempts because of his active pro-feminist stands and his vocal opposition to the deeply conservative but politically powerful Bohar Muslim priesthood in India. Farid, on the other hand, has been appointed a commissioner of gender equality in his country and has traveled widely, lecturing on Islamic liberation theology and the resources within that tradition for critical thinking, for religious pluralism, and for the full equality of women. Born into extreme poverty, he discovered early the solidarity of the poor across religious and racial boundaries at the everyday level of survival. He went on to discover in the struggle against apartheid a solidarity that was political, multi-religious, and powerful.

Ze'ev Falk was rector of the Seminary of Judaic Studies in Jerusalem. An Orthodox rabbi and scholar, Ze'ev struggled within his community of faith for a liberation of women and their religious practices rooted in Torah.

The parents of *Tavivat Puntarigvivat* fled China in the face of the Japanese invasion and settled in Bangkok, where Tavi would first become educated in economics at the prestigious Tammasat University. It left him curiously empty and still searching. He turned to the study of religion and eventually became, for a while, a *bhikkhu* (a Buddhist monk) in poverty-stricken northeast Thailand. There he was fed, both literally and symbolically, by the poor, some of whom also sold their daughters into prostitution. That was an unexpected education and one that continues to haunt him. Today, Tavi chairs the Comparative Religion Graduate Program at Mahidol University in Bangkok.

Mutombo Nkulu-N'Sengha was born in what in 1959 was still called the Belgian Congo. He was educated by the Catholic Church, first in the Congo and then in Rome at the Gregorian. Today, he teaches at Temple University in Philadelphia, where he received his doctorate. Besides his mother tongue of Kiluba, he speaks five other African languages; he writes and lectures in English, Italian, French, and Spanish. Growing up in the 1960s in the Congo, he experienced directly the anti-colonial struggles of his people and learned about violence and oppression when our own CIA arranged for the assassination of Patrice Lumumba, the first democratically elected prime minister of the Congo, who was deemed dangerous by the United States because of his socialist sympathies. About this Mutombo says today, "having lived under the dictatorship of Mobutu [who then came into power], the issue of social justice became a focal concern of my life and my thought."

Liu Xiaogan was born in 1947, two years before the founding of the People's Republic of China. His father was a clerk in the Red Army. During the Cultural Revolution of the late 1960s, he and his sister, both intellectuals, were sent by the government to be reeducated by the peasants of Inner Mongolia. What he learned there was how very difficult life "at the bottom" is, a fact that he would not forget as he returned to finish his doctoral level work at Beijing University. During the tragedy at Tian'anmen Square, he was doing postgraduate work at Harvard. He did not return to China and today teaches at the National University of Singapore.

Christopher Ronwanien:te Jocks teaches at Dartmouth College. He was born into the working-class culture of southern California where his Iroquois father served in the military and his Irish Catholic mother (a social activist and idealist) dropped out of college in the early 1970s for marriage and motherhood. It was there that Chris learned a haunting lesson (perhaps his life's "vision"). He saw a double degradation, each of which he thinks are closely related. He saw the despoiling of the land in the mad dash for real estate and profits. And he witnessed the slow dissent of his mother into deep depression, perhaps a result of her isolated life as a housewife and as a person of "the sixties," cast into adulthood in the obligatory normalcy of the seventies. Whatever could not be put into money terms had no value. Chris went a different direction, back to his roots in the cultures of our country's First Nations.

And then there is me, *John Raines*. White, male, and born into considerable class privilege, I was given what at the time was considered the best, most demanding, and selective of educations. But I got a second education I wasn't supposed to receive when I faced the arbitrary power of Southern white judges in the early 1960s who found the activities of Civil Rights workers worthy of jail. Up North, "my kind" had the power. Down South, "their kind" had the power and used that power to send us to jail. That began my lifelong interest in how power works and how privilege disguises from itself its relationship to power by way of rituals of (usually male) deservedness. I did those rituals—the right degrees, the right sports, the right clubs, the easy banter among privileged peers. I entered the space of recognition and social regard I was supposed to. But I carried memories with me of what our country looks like and lives like when looked at and lived from below. Those experiences as a Civil Rights worker stayed with me and began a journey that has brought me to this book.

There is one further explanation the reader is entitled to. It has to do with the dedication of this book. My mother is one of the women. Helen Latta is the other: She was the governess my parents hired to help raise me. I was the fourth child; ours was a socially prominent and necessarily busy family in Minneapolis, Minnesota, in the 1940s. My birth mother had her hands full and needed help. Helen was a middle-aged single woman, and she raised me as her own. I was lucky enough to have two mothers for a while.

For Further Reading

What Men Owe to Women: Men's Voices from World Religions, edited by John C. Raines and Daniel C. Maguire (Albany: SUNY Press, 2001). This volume featuring ten scholars of world religions is the basis, for the most part, of the present book. It is scholarly and fully argued.

Why Religion Matters: The Fate of the Human Spirit in an Age of Disbelief, by Huston Smith (New York: HarperCollins, 2001). A trenchant criticism of relativism and consumerism and a well-argued defense that religion remains an essential resource in the struggle for a humane future.

Feminism and World Religions, edited by Arvind Sharma and Katherine K. Young (McGill Studies in the History of Religions; Albany: SUNY Press, 1999), is a discussion by scholars of world religions about how the feminist critique enriches our grasp on the heritage of the sacred.

Sacred Choices: The Right to Contraception and Abortion in Ten World Religions, by Daniel C. Maguire (Minneapolis: Fortress Press, 2001), does what its title indicates and discloses the positive resources in world religions for women's reproductive choice.

Good Sex: Feminist Perspectives from the World's Religions, edited by Patricia Beattie Jung, Mary E. Hunt, and Radhika Balakrishnan (New Brunswick, N.J.: Rutgers University Press, 2001). This book documents positive resources in religious traditions concerning erotic justice, and the voice that speaks is the voice of women.

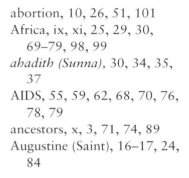

Index